Right Down THE Middle
THE RALPH TERRY STORY

Ralph Terry
62 W.S.
MVP

M
[L]

Ralph Terry *with* John Wooley

müllerhaus
[LEGACY]

TULSA

ACCOLADES FOR
RIGHT DOWN THE MIDDLE

Participants in major league sports like to reminisce. Often they enhance their performances or get few of the details right, with two exceptions: pro golfers and major league pitchers. The golfer chronicles every stroke he takes during a 72-hole tournament and can relate it with total accuracy. The pitcher, even after the passing of decades, remembers the slider low and on the outside corner to the cleanup hitter and the fastball high and tight to move the batter off the plate. Their total recall is from the first pitch in the game to the last out.

Ralph Terry excelled in both sports.

Two of Ralph's pitches were the last in classic seventh-game World Series matchups between great teams. Along with other "inside baseball" stories, the reader will go into the clubhouse, dugout, participants' minds and, best of all, onto the pitcher's mound where two of the most exciting endings in baseball history took place.

> – *Ralph's teammate* **TONY KUBEK**, *1957 American*
> *League Rookie of the Year, four-time All-Star, and*
> *Ford C. Frick Award-winning TV broadcaster*

Ralph Terry was never flashy. He didn't use gimmicks or tricks—he was a blue-collar pitcher who knew exactly where he wanted the ball to go and how to get it there. That was his game, and when he was on the mound, he owned it. An acquaintance for many years… and a friend for life.

> – *Ralph's teammate* **BOBBY RICHARDSON**, *eight-time All-Star, five-time Gold Glove Award winner, and 1960 World Series MVP.*

Ralph Terry's story is one of the great ones in all of sports. Having pitched two seventh games in a World Series, this world champion is one of the true legends of baseball.

> – **CLIFF RICHEY**, *America's former No. 1 tennis player and founding member of Celebrity Players' Golf Tour*

In my sport, golf, Ralph Terry became a top professional and earned the respect of the greatest golfer of all time, Jack Nicklaus. This book tells the story of why the greats in baseball respect Ralph and how he became the MVP of the 1962 World Series. It's a redemption story, an American comeback story, and a New York Yankees story.

> – **JIM MCLEAN**, *multiple PGA award winner and one of the world's leading golf instructors*

Every member of the "baby boom generation" should read this book. *Right Down the Middle* transports you to the time when baseball was America's sport, Ralph's teams set the standard for excellence, and each of us dreamed of playing for or against the New York Yankees.

> – **DAN REA**, *host of* NightSide with Dan Rea, *WBZ Radio, Boston*

Müllerhaus Publishing Arts, Inc.
DBA Müllerhaus Legacy
5200 South Yale Ave, Penthouse | Tulsa, Oklahoma 74135
www.MullerhausLegacy.com

Printed in the United States

ISBN-13: 978-0-6927880-8-0
LCCN: 2016916289

Every effort has been made to trace the ownership of all copyrighted material
included in this publication. Any errors that may have occured are inadvertent
and will be corrected in subsequent additions, provided notification is sent
to the publisher.

Cover Design by Douglas Miller
Interior Design by Laura Hyde
Photo Acquisition by Jim Russell
Cover Photographs © The National Baseball Hall of Fame Library, Cooperstown, NY.

müllerhaus [LEGACY]

THE CRAFT OF STORYTELLING. Great stories surround us. Every family, organization and community is steeped in memories of triumph and loss, sacrifice and love. But rarely are these stories woven together in a way that captivates this generation and inspires the next. That's where we can help. Whether on printed page or in digital media, Müllerhaus Legacy guides you in preserving and sharing your stories with a commitment that matches your passion. To be craftsmen in the trade of storytelling we've learned we must first be confidants in the art of listening. Our uncompromising standards of personal care, professional service and attention to detail will make your experience with us its own magnificent adventure. Your stories are your legacy. Telling your stories is ours. | **MullerhausLegacy.com**

Thanks to John Wooley and Jim Russell for their tireless effort. Their enthusiasm was amazing!

To Tommy Byrne, Allie Reynolds, Jim Konstanty, Spud Chandler, Jim Turner, Eddie Lopat and especially John Sain, some of the best pitchers in the history of the game, for sharing their knowledge, wisdom and experience with a young pitcher.

Thanks to Jerry Volpe for getting me started in professional golf.

Thanks to some of the most brilliant teachers in the game of golf for all their help and friendship—Lew Worsham, Carl Lohren, Joe Norwood, Mac O'Grady and Jim McLean.

To my golfing pals in Larned and to the Great Bend "Mafia" Gang.

Thanks to long-time friends—Danny Collins, Bruce Vaughn, Mike Wegner, Dan Nolde, Kelly Eastes, Mike Nickel, Keith Ceislak, Joe Falco and Bill McAlister and four very special people: Dennis Walters, Dan Rea, Cliff Richey and Sean Thayer.

To my brother "Jake," who looked after me when we were little and would always slice the hamburger and piece of pie "Right Down the Middle." One of the most honest and fairest-minded men I have ever known. Love you, "Bro"!

To my teammates who made my story possible; so many are gone. We loved each other like brothers.

To the Yankee fans who never gave up on me after losing the 7th game in Pittsburgh. They're the best fans in the world!

Thanks to my wife, Tanya. What a trooper! She went through it all—the sadness and the elation—and never wavered. And to our sons, Raif and Gabe, for making us proud parents.

– All my love, Ralph

I'd like to use my portion of the dedication to acknowledge the importance Jim Russell, a good old friend, played in seeing *Right Down the Middle* become a reality. It was Jim who contacted both Ralph and me about doing a book, and he did it for the purest of motives: He simply was driven to get Ralph's story down on paper and preserved for future generations. If this were a movie, Jim would be its producer. We would not and could not have done it without him.

And if I may presume on behalf of Ralph and Jim, I'd like to dedicate this book to Chelsea, Oklahoma, the hometown we all share, as well as to the long-ago baseball diamonds where we joyfully spent hour upon dusty hour—one of us with far more success than the other two.

– John W.

TABLE OF CONTENTS

00

INTRODUCTION

People sometimes ask me if I've ever been nervous or scared in a baseball game. When they do, I can honestly tell them that it only happened once, and I can even give them the exact date—August 6, 1956.

A few days earlier, the New York Yankees had called me up from their Triple-A affiliate in Denver, where I was 11-2. The Yankees were in Detroit for a weekend series with the Tigers, and Casey Stengel, our manager, wanted to start me in the second game. The night before, Whitey Ford had had a rare spell of ineffectiveness, facing only five batters before being pulled for Rip Coleman with one out in the first inning; the Tigers had gone on to win it 10-4, with Billy Hoeft throwing a complete game.

The next day, I was sitting in the clubhouse before the game, and Casey was sitting at his desk. There wasn't a separate office for the visiting manager at Detroit, so his desk was right over in the corner of the locker room, in the same room as all us ballplayers.

The phone on the desk rang, and Casey answered. It was George Weiss, the Yankees' general manager, and while I wasn't trying to listen in, I could hear their conversation.

"You've got to change your starting pitcher today," Weiss told him. "You need to switch to Bob Turley."

"Wait a minute," Stengel said. "Who's running this team—me or you?"

"No, no, Casey. It's not like that. This is going to be the Game of the Week on CBS, with [announcers] Dizzy Dean and Buddy Blattner. It's a big deal, and we want to put a name out there."

I could understand that. Turley was a two-time all-star and one of the hardest throwers in the majors at the time. Some were calling him the next Bob Feller, who was just then in the last year of his Hall of Fame career. Baseball fans around the country knew who Turley was; they had no reason to know *me*, a rookie just up from Triple-A.

So Turley pitched, and we lost the game on a blown save by Don Larsen. The next day, Johnny Kucks started the final game of the series. We lost that one, too, even though Mickey Mantle hit three home runs over that weekend—two in the second game, one in the third, the last one a monster shot that hit the Briggs Stadium light tower just about where Reggie Jackson's famous homer landed in the 1971 All-Star Game. But the Tigers' Al Kaline hit three, too, and we left Detroit with a six-game losing streak.

Our next stop was Fenway Park in Boston. Even with the six-game skid, we were still in first place. But third-place Boston, a game and a half behind the Cleveland Indians, was riding a six-game *winning* streak. The Red Sox were still 8 and a half games out of first, but their surge had stirred up their fan base. Plus, the great Yankee-Red Sox rivalry was always good for getting big numbers through the turnstiles. So maybe it wasn't that surprising that we were met that Monday night by the largest turnout at Fenway since Boston's 1948 playoff game with Cleveland. Officially, 35,923 people were in the stands for the game, which meant that about 25 times the population of my hometown of Chelsea, Oklahoma, would be right there watching me make my regular season, major league debut. And most of them would not be friendly.

I don't doubt all of that had something to do with my pre-game jitters, but there were other factors, too. I hadn't pitched for a while, and I was always worried about getting rusty. I really wanted to be the guy who put a stop to our losing streak, but it wouldn't be easy. I was up against their ace, Tommy Brewer, who was 15-3 at the time.

Whatever the reasons, I was getting more and more rattled the closer it got to game time. In those days, pitchers would warm up between the dugout and home plate, on the third-base and first-base side. So I was throwing before the game, warming up, and I was *bouncing* the ball up there. I had nothing in my throws. The crowd was buzzing, and I couldn't look up at the stands. I actually felt physically weak.

I remember thinking, "What the hell is going on?" It was *weird.*

Then the game began. Billy Martin, batting leadoff for us, doubled to right field and went to third on a wild pitch from Brewer. But Hank Bauer and Mickey struck out, and Yogi Berra flied out to center, so Martin was stranded. No score.

In the home half of the first inning, I finally got out to the mound at Fenway, in front of that noisy crowd, and watched as the first batter, Billy Goodman, stepped up to the plate. He was a left-handed hitter and a good one, with an average at the time of over .300.

I looked in for the sign from Yogi. Putting one finger down, he held his mitt right in the middle of the plate.

"A fastball down the middle?" I thought. "That's *Billy Goodman* up there. He's a good hitter. Shouldn't I throw him a curve or something on the first pitch?"

I could almost hear Yogi's voice in my head: "C'mon, kid. Right down the middle." That mitt didn't move.

Keeping my eye on it, I wound up and let go, and the ball split the heart of the plate. A fastball, right down the middle.

"Strike one!" called the ump.

And that was it. Just like a cloud dissipating, the nervousness left me. It was like opening kickoff back when I'd played high school football in Chelsea. I was in the game. That was all it took.

No matter where I played after that, in the World Series or anywhere else, I was never afraid again.

01

COW-PASTURE BALL

The day I saw my first ballgame, I didn't even know what a baseball *was*. I'd never heard of any baseball players, not even Babe Ruth.

I must've been four or five years old, which would've made it 1940 or '41. But I can still remember that Sunday summer afternoon out in the back of the Bitter Creek schoolhouse, where a couple of section lines crossed. There was a diamond laid out there with a little backstop and cattle grazing in the outfield. No fences. Some people from the county had come out on road graders and cleaned up the field, which included scraping up a lot of cow manure. Someone else had filled gunny sacks with grain, sewed 'em up, and put them out for first, second, and third base. They weren't tied down or anything. As I remember, the pitching mound was a two-by-four with a piece of Model A tire stretched over it and nailed down to make the pitching rubber.

People came from all over to watch the game. They came in wagons drawn by horses and mules. Some rode in on horseback, others in Model A Fords. After a while, up rolled a flatbed truck from the nearby town of Pryor, a bunch of ballplayers sitting in the back. They jumped off, started playing catch, and pretty soon the game was underway.

The field where Ralph saw his first baseball game, nine miles east of his hometown of Chelsea, Oklahoma, on the southeast corner of the intersection of county roads NS 431 and EW 370.

My dad was pitching for our side. Just about the only thing I recall about the game itself is that some guy hit a screaming liner right back at him and—smack!—he caught it. That really impressed me.

We lived not far from there, around the towns of Chelsea, Big Cabin, and Adair, halfway between the Bitter Creek and Council Grove schools. Dad, Mom, my older brother John—we called him Jake or J.C.—and I all lived in a one-room log cabin with a dirt floor. It sat on forty acres of land, next to the acreage where my grandfather on my dad's side lived. It was granddad's land.

I had been born in that cabin on January 9, 1936. The doctor who delivered me came out of Adair, so he wrote "Adair" on my birth certificate. Actually, we were closer to Big Cabin, which is why most of

RALPH'S MOTHER
Mrs. Erma Terry

RALPH'S FATHER
Frank Terry

Ralph with his uncle John "Baldy" Terry and his older brother John, known by the family as Jake or J.C.

RALPH'S GRANDMOTHER
Mrs. Rose Terry with Ralph

my biographical information—including what's on my baseball cards—lists that town as my birthplace. Chelsea didn't come into the picture until I was in the fourth grade. That's when I enrolled in Chelsea Public School.

I was thinking the other day how the title of this book, *Right Down the Middle*, could also have applied to Jake and me in those days. We'd both been born toward the end of the Great Depression, a tough time for most of America but especially hard on people in Dust Bowl states like Oklahoma. Even with both of our parents working, it was tough. The best meal of our day was the school lunch we got at Chelsea, although Mom, who worked in town at Alvin Gliedt's café, would sometimes bring us home a hamburger and a piece of pie. Whenever that happened, the rules were very clear: Jake would cut the slice of pie and the burger in half, and I'd get to pick which half was mine. Do I need to tell you that he was scrupulous about making his cut right down the middle?

Both Dad and Mom did whatever they could to keep us clothed and fed, and that included running a couple of beer bars, one up at what the locals referred to as Ten-Mile Corner in Afton, Oklahoma, and another outside of Vinita, Oklahoma, where Highways 66 and 69 split off. Because of its location, it was called the Y-Inn.

Both of those joints were pretty rough, with beer in the front, booze and crap games in the back, and always the threat of a fight breaking out—especially at the Y-Inn, and especially on Saturday nights, when the biggest games went on and people were blowing off steam before going back to work on Monday. Dad was his own bouncer, but one night it was Mom who broke things up. When the combatants started tearing up the bar, she went to the back and came out with a pistol. She leveled it at them with both her hands shaking, and you talk about people getting the hell out of there. They knew it was her place, and when they saw her holding a gun on them with shaking hands, they straightened up in a heartbeat.

I remember the bootleggers, who'd drive by in cars that ran low to the ground because of all the bottles they carried. Sometimes those guys would be the most respected members of their communities. I also remember the man who used to run the nickelodeon—the jukebox—in the Y-Inn, old Ray Culp. He'd come in to take care of things and get back the quarters and nickels and dimes that had been marked. If they were marked, that meant they'd been put in the nickelodeon by management to stimulate business, so they weren't part of the take. Sometimes, he'd put a few of those coins back in and play a little music.

Dad didn't drink or smoke, and I've never been much of a drinker myself. Most of the time, two in an evening has been my limit. I've been drunk maybe three or four times in my life (most of those times with Mickey Mantle, because he was fun to drink with). I don't know if I'm that way because Dad was a teetotaler, or because of what I saw when I went in to help him clean up at those joints he ran. There'd be men I really liked slumped at the bar or a table or lying around shitfaced, money falling out of their pockets, slurring their words, throwing up. The nice guys I knew had turned themselves into slobbering ugly drunks, and I've never forgotten seeing them that way. I guess you'd say I was scared straight, like those kids they take into prison to show them what'll happen if they don't change their ways.

I imagine running those dives took its toll on Dad and Mom. Just before I turned six, we packed up and took off, leaving the bar business behind. Heading west in Dad's '35 Chevy, we were bound for Oregon, where his aunt Loni Bell lived. We made it as far as Salt Lake City before our money ran out. Dad was a Mason, so we stopped at the Masonic Lodge and stayed for three or four days. His fellow Masons passed the hat and raised something like 75 dollars for us, which was a pretty good amount of money at the time. So with that new grubstake, we set off again, stopping next at Northern California, around Fresno, where we spent some time working in the fields like migrant workers, out there in the mud picking up English walnuts. We ate about half of what we picked up. They tasted good, and we were hungry.

From there, we traveled to Oregon—and I hated it, mostly because it rained all the time. Aunt Loni and Uncle Perry Bell lived in Springfield, Oregon, near Eugene, and the folks dropped us off there and headed on to Portland, where they both worked in the Kaiser shipyards. Pearl Harbor had already happened by that time, because the U.S. was building ships and planes and tanks as quickly as it could, and the need for civilian labor was great.

I turned six just about a month after the Pearl Harbor attack, and I remember going to the first grade in Springfield, which meant I started there in the fall of '42. Patriotic fervor was running high that year, with lots of men and women queuing up at the recruiting stations to join the military and fight the Axis. Because Dad was working in the defense industry, building ships, I'm sure he would've gotten a deferment, but he went ahead and enlisted in the Navy and shipped out. After J.C. and I finished a year of school at Springfield, Mom moved us back to Oklahoma, where we lived on my grandparents' farm.

Everyone worked then. Even before we'd gone to Oregon, I was running a sulky rake—a horse-drawn hay-rake with a seat in the middle. That horse would just fly along, and I'd have to not only drive her but also dump the rake with my foot when it got full, and I could barely reach it. Even though I started doing it when I was only five, I never had a serious accident on it, which made me luckier than a lot of my peers in those days. You'd see a lot of farm kids walking around with their skulls caved in from being kicked by a horse or a cow, or sporting jagged barbed-wire scars, all kinds of stuff. Besides running the sulky rake, I was pitching hay and bucking bales and hoeing corn, handling feed and calves and hogs, and milking cows. They put your ass to work at an early age back then.

LIFELONG BUDDIES
Ralph Terry and his best friend, Galen Hudspeth
(right), played high school football together.

Back in Oklahoma, I went to the second grade at Council Grove, which we called Bugscuffle. Our teacher was Mrs. Edmonds. She was wonderful. There were eight grades together in the schoolhouse, each grade seated in its own row, and she had a big blackboard where she'd write all the assignments for the different classes. I was a good student, and because of the way she taught, I could do eighth-grade math when I was in the second grade. It was a great way to learn. When you're young, you can learn so much so quickly, and I ate it up. Mrs. Edmonds skipped me from the second to the third grade while I was there, so when I started at Chelsea, I was a fourth-grader rather than a third-grader. After my first-grade year in Oregon and my year at Bugscuffle, I would stay until graduation in Chelsea Public Schools.

* * * *

The ancient basswood tree Ralph and Galen Hudspeth used to climb still stands on the southeast corner of 10th & Vine Streets in their hometown of Chelsea.

At Chelsea, you went to McIntosh School through the fifth grade and then to another building, Longfellow, for the sixth, seventh, and eighth. I never really played any baseball until I got over to Longfellow. I was into *football*. So was my best friend, Galen Hudspeth, who was part-Cherokee Indian and about a year and a half older than me. We'd collect old magazines and write-ups about football players like Bob Fenimore, a great athlete from Woodward, Oklahoma, who'd gone on to become an All-American at Oklahoma A&M College (now Oklahoma State University).

Most of us had nicknames back then. Another friend, Travis McSpadden, started calling Galen "Hunchy" after the All-American quarterback out of Indiana University, Bob "Hunchy" Hoernschemeyer. Galen was a quarterback, too—he could really throw the ball, even when he was young.

As a kid, I was red-haired and freckle-faced, so they called me Booger Red. I didn't know it at the time, but I guess it came from the famous bronc rider of the late 1800s, Sam Privett, who popularized that nickname. As I grew out of the red hair and freckles, they shortened it to "Boog." Much later, when I was pitching professionally, sometimes I'd hear a person in the stands yell, "Hey, Boog!" I'd always know that was somebody from Chelsea, somebody from home.

When I was in the fifth grade, Galen and I and some of the other kids started watching the town team play baseball at McSpadden Park, just across the street from McIntosh. I don't know if this had anything to do with our attraction to the park, but I remember when William Boyd, who played Hopalong Cassidy in the movies, came to McSpadden Park with his horse, Topper. This was a few years before Boyd, who grew up in Tulsa, would get rich selling his old cowboy movies to television, but he was still a big star to us kids.

Every little whistle-stop on the map had a baseball team then, made up of local merchants and other adults who would come out and play against other town teams. In the fifth grade, Galen and I began to throw a baseball around some, and after a while we started going out to the park and shagging balls whenever the town team took batting practice. Then, when they had games, we'd hang around and chase down foul balls. Every time you brought one back, they'd give you a dime.

A lot of things happened in the sixth grade. First of all, I moved up to Longfellow, and I found out pretty fast that the two big activities for boys at recess were dodge ball and baseball. Galen, who could throw a baseball as well as he could a football, started pitching, and I started catching him. No mask or anything. You played as far as you could behind the batter, and if someone tipped a foul back at you, you just ducked your head and tried to get out of the way.

Mrs. Juanita Herrold was our sixth-grade teacher, a great teacher, and she let us listen to the 1946 World Series games between the Cardinals and the Red Sox. I think that's where I really got the fever for baseball. We used to listen a lot to Harry Caray calling the Cardinals games on the radio.

I was in my sixth-grade year when my folks divorced. At the time Dad got discharged from the Navy and came back home, he and Mom had been apart for four years, and for whatever reason they decided they liked it that way. It might be hard for today's kids to understand, but then there was a kind of stigma that came with being from a divorced family. I remember wanting to excel, to make something of myself and rise above my family situation. Meanwhile, Mom had to work to support J.C. and me. Eventually, she married Charlie Dawes, who had a good job with Shell Pipeline, and they ended up with three kids of their own, Billy, Susie, and Mike.

In the seventh and eighth grades, my final two years at Longfellow, I started playing more baseball. When summer came along, we'd go down to McSpadden Park and play there. They didn't have Little League in those days, so we'd make up our own teams, sometimes putting kids from the east side of town against the west side, one part of Chelsea against another. One of my most vivid memories of those times is seeing little Don Delozier riding in on his cow to play ball with us. She had a cowbell around her neck, and he had a rope with a weight on the end that he tied onto her when he turned her out into the park. She'd graze contentedly while we played ball, and then he'd ride her back home.

Looking back, I believe my eighth grade year, 1948-49, was when I started taking baseball more seriously. I began paying attention to the Chelsea High School Green Dragons team, which had a lot of good players then. Pat Delozier was a really good catcher, and Lefty Parks had a great curveball. There were the two Harrell brothers, J.R. and Leroy, and Bob Bard, who could both pitch and play infield. Tom Younger had a good arm. Norm Stanley threw hard. Ken Judd played centerfield. They went to the state tournament that year and lost to Byng in the finals. I'd say they were an inspiration to me, especially since I'd be in high school the following year.

In the summer of 1949, at the age of 13, I caught for the first time in American Legion ball. Then, when I started the ninth grade, I became the regular catcher for the Chelsea High School team, which still had a lot of those players from the year before.

I liked catching fine, but I burned to pitch, too. I'd had the itch for a long time, but I'd gotten it especially bad that summer, after the town team had started letting me throw batting practice. I was blessed with a good arm, and being a catcher, I'd had the opportunity to really study pitching. To me, catching was a beautiful position. It showed you the way a curveball could bend around the corner of the plate and make a guy swing and miss, the effectiveness of a ball thrown high and tight. Catching, I think, prepared me for pitching and made me a better pitcher. From behind the plate, I saw things that batters had trouble with. I saw how you could get even good hitters out by doing things like changing speeds after two strikes. I just *got* it.

Throughout the season, I'd been bugging our coach, Rupert Cross, about letting me pitch. Every time, he'd turn me down, telling me they needed me more behind the plate and stuff like that.

Finally, the last game of the season came along. It was Senior Day. Rupert could be pretty hard on his players, and by this time they were all tired. The team wasn't going anywhere, either. So on the day of the final game, all of the seniors took off for Grand Lake or Noel, Missouri—I can't remember which of those nearby getaway areas they went to, but I know they all left.

Our final opponent of the year was Foyil, nine miles down the road. I guess Rupert didn't have anybody else, or I finally wore him down, or both, but he told me I could start the game against Foyil. I don't remember who caught me, but I went out there and pitched a one-hitter, striking out 21 men. Buck Rose, a friend of mine, hit a grounder to deep short and beat it out; that's they only hit the Foyil team got off me.

I was throwing sidearm then, because I'd read a book by Ewell Blackwell, the big sidearmer, and I figured that was the way to do it. I didn't have a curveball or anything else. Fastballs were all I gave 'em.

We won by a big margin, and I helped myself out by hitting a three-run double and a grand-slam home run that hit the Foyil High School ag building out in left center field.

Afterwards, Rupert said, "Well, I guess you *can* pitch."

It was the best day I'd ever had in my life.

02

A BASEBALL TOWN—ST. LOUIS

A month or so after he'd gotten the only hit off me in the Foyil game, Buck Rose went with me on a big major league adventure. A couple of his cousins had come down to visit from East St. Louis, and when they were getting ready to return home, we made arrangements to ride up there with them. I went to my mom and dad and managed to get twenty dollars from each of them, so I was set. We rode up, carrying our little knapsacks, and his cousins dropped us off at Forest Park, where we slept, right out there in the open. We took trolleys across town for, as I remember it, fifteen cents, went up to the Point of Rocks area way out in north St. Louis, and then came back and stopped downtown, where we saw the Garrett Theatre Follies, a famous burlesque show, with a bunch of sailors around us in the audience. We really got a kick out of being there.

What we were really in town for, though, was to see the Cardinals and the Pittsburgh Pirates play a three-game series. And we did. We watched Howie Pollet pitch for the Cardinals, with Enos Slaughter playing right field. Pirates star Ralph Kiner hit a home run. We saw Stan Musial, Marty Marion, Red Schoendist, Del Rice, Rip Repulski, Jabbo Jablonski, Red Munger, and Al Brazle, all guys we were familiar with from listening to the games on the radio. Now we were seeing all these bigger-than-life names in person, playing the game that made them stars to us. I learned a lot by just watching them go through their paces at Sportsman's Park, and being there to see those three games gave me an even bigger dose of the baseball bug.

I caught again my sophomore year for the Green Dragons, with Galen doing most of the pitching, and between my sophomore and junior year, I started as a pitcher in American Legion ball. It was early summer, 1951, and the St. Louis Cardinals were holding a tryout camp in Pryor, right down the road. The night before, I'd pitched a Legion game against Pryor, striking out 21 men and winning 4-2. Even though I'd thrown a complete game the night before, I decided I'd go out to the camp and give it a shot, just to see how I'd stack up.

Back in those days, a lot of guys were signed out of those camps. Because the major league teams didn't have the scouting bureaus, and the draft, and all the stuff they have now, the camps were an important way they had of evaluating prospects. Lots of young ballplayers would always show up, hoping to beat the odds and get signed to a contract; when I showed up in the early morning at that camp in Pryor, I'll bet there were already more than 100 there. Most of them were older than me, college or semipro players. Me, I was only 15. And since you had to be 18 to legally participate in the camp, I lied about my age to get in.

Every pitcher there got to come out and pitch to nine batters while a scout watched from just behind the mound. I remember the two Cardinal scouts who were there that day: Freddie Hahn and Runt Marr, two baseball veterans who always traveled together in a big Buick.

The camp started on a Saturday morning. When my turn came to pitch, I went out there and struck out eight of the nine hitters I faced, throwing all fastballs. The only one I didn't strike out hit a little popup to the catcher. After fanning the ninth guy, I flipped the ball to the scout and left.

The next day, they called out the names of five people who were being offered contracts by the Cardinals based on their camp tryouts. My name was one of the five. If I'd been three years older, I could've signed up for the majors then. But because I was only 15, and the camp was for players 18 and older, I wasn't eligible.

I knew then, though, maybe for the first time, that I might actually be able to make it as a baseball player.

* * * *

I don't want to go any further without saying something more about the men on the Chelsea town team. Not only did they let me pitch batting practice to them as I was growing up, some of them also went well out of their way to help nurture whatever aptitude I had for baseball. I especially remember the town veterinarian, Dr. Frank Hester, and Chelsea's dentist, Dr. Charles Kouri. They'd help in so many ways. I remember Dr. Kouri taking some of us high school boys to Tulsa several times to watch the Tulsa Oilers, a Double-A affiliate of the Cincinnati Reds at the time.

Dr. Kouri knew people, and I don't know whether it was because of him or because of a column the *Tulsa Tribune*'s sports editor, Jack Charvat, wrote about this 15-year-old from Chelsea who had been striking a lot of guys out, but for whatever reason I got to pitch batting practice a couple of times for the Oilers in the Double A Texas League. The first time, the old second baseman Al Vincent was in his last year as manager, and they had Ed Bailey, the catcher, and future stars like Joe Adcock and Johnny Temple on the team. I'd throw it up there and, boy, they'd whack it. It was great.

Next year, when Joe Schultz was managing, I went back down there and threw batting practice again. I saw a lot of good players on the field at old Texas League Park, including my future teammate and roommate

Bullet Bob Turley, who came through with San Antonio. Bobby Bragan was managing the Fort Worth Cats, and I remember him working with Rex Barney back in '51. Only three years earlier, Barney had won 15 games for the Brooklyn Dodgers, but he'd lost his control. He threw real hard, but he was wild, and despite Bragan's best efforts, Barney would be out of baseball by the end of the '52 season.

Because of Dr. Kouri and others, I got to watch all these pro ballplayers, to study them and see how they operated. He was a big help to me, and I was glad later on to acknowledge his influence on my career by giving him my 1963 World Series ring.

* * * *

As I wrote earlier, Mom's second husband Charlie Dawes worked for Shell Pipeline, and he knew another man from Chelsea named Robards, who was the father of a friend of mine named Paul Robards. Old Man Robards was a pipeline inspector, and he got me a job that summer working a pipeline job in the nearby Osage Hills. Once again, I had to claim that I was 18 in order to be employed, but I was pretty big for my age, so I was able to get by with it.

I was one of the right-of-way crew, working on a ten-inch line, and it was almost like being a combat engineer. We'd clean out a 45-yard right-of-way, fell timbers, and then take those timbers and build bridges across the creeks. Sometimes we'd be in mud up to our necks, with cables zinging all around us, building bridges they could run Caterpillars across. It was dangerous damn work.

The crew manager was a guy named Punk Musser from Chandler, Oklahoma. He'd played a little baseball, mostly as a catcher, and during the lunch hour he'd get an axe handle and I'd throw rocks to him for batting practice. He'd hit those rocks—bang!—with that axe handle. We'd have a lot of fun doing that, and we needed the breaks, since we were working seventy hours a week. I made a dollar and a quarter an hour, with time and a half after 40 hours, so I was making 100 or 125 bucks a week. I sent it home to pay for my school expenses the next year, blue jeans and books and all of that.

The next summer, between my junior and senior year at Chelsea High, I got a call from a man named I.T. "Mutt" Hocker, who was the head of the Baxter Springs Whiz Kids, a team in the Ban Johnson League. Named after a former president of the American League, the Ban Johnson organization was based in Kansas City, with teams in towns throughout Kansas and Missouri, and their rosters were full of college-level players. It was a step up from American Legion ball—basically, a summer league for college players. If you made one of the teams, management would find you a summer job so you could afford to play baseball for them and still retain your amateur status. I tried out, made the Whiz Kids—the same team Mickey Mantle had played for a few years earlier—and had a good season. I was 16, the youngest player in the league, and I really progressed during that summer of '52, learning more about baseball and pitching than I ever had before. It was during that time of learning and playing that I really began to be scouted.

I really was coached then, too. The Whiz Kids were managed by an old guy named Barney Barnett, a miner who'd been working with base-ball teams in the area for decades. It would be his last year to manage, as well as the final year of his life. He'd coached Mickey, of course, and he'd had the future major league catcher Sherm Lollar before that. He turned out a lot of good players, and I was happy to help get him installed in the Kansas Baseball Hall of Fame in 2012, sixty years after his death.

His son, Barney Jr., was a big guy, about 6' 5", who'd pitched a lit-tle in the low minors before World War II and then been drafted by the Chicago Cardinals, predecessor to the NFL's Arizona Cardinals, out of

Northeastern Oklahoma A&M in '47. He'd played pro football for three years. In between his baseball and football jobs, he'd served in the European theater as a paratrooper. Because he'd worked in the mines like his dad, he could handle dynamite, and they'd drop him behind enemy lines so he could blow stuff up. He'd been on Normandy during D-Day, and he used to tell us about getting a beachhead established with the rest of the troops, only to find a concrete pillbox in the way of the trucks. I still remember how he told it:

"My officer came to me and said, 'Barnett, you think you could blow that thing up?' 'Sure, Lieutenant,' I said, and I threw a couple of sticks of dynamite into it. Turned out to be an ammo dump. The concrete and everything just blew sky-high, and everybody was running for cover, ducking the chunks of stuff falling out of the sky. That thing must've gone off for 15 minutes."

Back in August of '95, when Mickey died, I called Barney Jr. up. He was in a kind of rest home over there in Baxter Springs, and I asked him if he was going to the funeral down in Dallas.

He said, "I don't have a way. I don't get around much."

"Well," I said, "I'm picking you up, and we're going together."

So I went over and got him and we drove down. We sat together in the service with the baseball commissioner, Bud Selig, and old Yankees Jerry Coleman and Andy Carey, just behind the family. Bobby Richardson and Bob Costas spoke, and it was supposed to be an uplifting, happy occasion, but it was a real tear-jerker. It turned out to be very sad. Roy Clark sang "Yesterday, When I Was Young," and I heard later he said the only way he got through it without crying was to think about a banana split.

After the funeral, we were all gathered around outside, and there wasn't a dry eye in the group—except for Barney. He told us, "I don't know. Something's wrong with me. Ever since Normandy, when I saw guys all around me getting blown to bits, I haven't been able to cry."

Maybe his war experiences made the idea of bouncing back so important to him. When he was coaching us in Baxter Springs, that's what he drilled into our heads, over and over. "You've got to bounce back, bounce back, bounce back," he'd tell us. "If you make an error, bounce back. You've always got to come back. When you lose, you've got to come back and get the next one."

He really instilled that into my sixteen-year-old brain. I learned that the most important pitch was the next one, the most important game was the next one. Forget the past, and set your eyes on the future.

Years later, I asked him if he ever thought I'd make a big-league pitcher.

"Really, I didn't know," he said. "But Dad told me, 'If there's a God in heaven, he'll make it.'"

* * * *

While pitching for the Whiz Kids, I also worked a full-time job. Mutt Hocker got me on at Root Manufacturing Company, which made aluminum hulls for Toro lawn mowers. They'd come out of the smelter, and I'd put 'em on a lathe, and another guy would lower them down and grind them into shape. When he was done with each one, I'd pick it up, stack it, and fit another one onto the lathe. I made 35 dollars a week doing that, and it was hot, hard work. Then I'd play ball at night.

One of the Ban Johnson League teams was in Alba, a suburb of Joplin (which is where the Boyers—Cloyd, Ken, and my future Yankee teammate Clete—came from). Alba had a real good team then, and I had a good game against them, striking out 21 batters and almost throwing a no-hitter; the center fielder lost a fly ball in the lights and it dropped beside him. That was the only hit they got off me. There were two scouts in the park watching that game: Danny Doyle from the Red Sox and another guy from the White Sox whose name I've forgotten, a very tough guy with only one arm. I guess I made a pretty good impression, because it was after that game that I started really getting noticed. The Cardinals, who'd sponsored the tryout camp in Pryor the summer before, were one of the teams that began watching me. They had part-time scouts—birddogs, they were called—who'd go to the games and make reports: "Hey, there's a good player over here in Baxter Springs, and this is what he's doing." They kept track of me.

I went back to Chelsea High School in the fall for my senior year. I'd always played football and basketball as well as baseball. In those days, my friends and I were always playing sports, and we'd play whatever was in season. But things had changed between my junior and senior year. Not only were the big-league scouts keeping track of me, they were also giving me advice. And one of the things they told me was, "Do *not* play football. You're going to go pro and get a big bonus. But if you hurt your arm, it's over."

One afternoon a couple of weeks before school started, I was playing baseball at McSpadden Park in Chelsea, and Rupert Cross, who coached basketball and baseball as well as football for Chelsea, came by. He watched for a little while from behind the screen that separated the diamond from the bleachers, and then he hollered at me: "If you don't play football, you're not going to play baseball, either!"

I'd played football for him and the Chelsea Green Dragons all through high school; as far as my buddies and I were concerned, if you didn't play football, you didn't have a hair on your ass. We had good teams, and Rupert and I had a good rapport. He was a great, great football coach—but he was all football. It was his passion. All other sports, including baseball, were secondary to him, and while I didn't know for sure if he had been serious that day at McSpadden Park, I still had to weigh what he'd said against what the scouts were telling me.

I held out until just before football season started, sitting in study hall on the top floor of the school building and watching through the window every school day as the football team practiced on the field below. Finally, I just got bored with sitting there watching my buddies play ball. So I went out and joined the football team again.

The 1952-53 season was a good one for the Chelsea Green Dragons footballers. Late in September, we beat our heavily favored rivals from the Rogers County seat, the Claremore Zebras, by a score of 12-7 at McSpadden Park. I was lucky enough to score both touchdowns, the first one on a short down-and-out pass from Peavine Powell, and the second—in the final minutes of the game—on a longer down-and-out thrown to me by my running buddy Galen Hudspeth.

The *Chelsea Reporter* said that a record crowd was on hand to see the first Chelsea victory over Claremore in 26 years. It was such a big deal that school officials even called off all classes for Monday.

Then came a day before our last game of the season, when we were scheduled to play the Afton Eagles. Several of us were out there running back kicks. I grabbed one and took off down the field, getting by everyone but the last man, my teammate Sam Napier. He reached out, grabbed my shoulder pad, and hooked me. I spun around and landed on my right shoulder, dislocating it.

I played the whole game against Afton with my arm strapped to my side, blocking and playing in the backfield. And the number of big-league teams scouting me went from fifteen to about two.

* * * *

At the same time I was being scouted for baseball, I attracted the attention of the football coach from Oklahoma A&M, Jenning Bryan Whitworth. He was an old wrestler with cauliflower ears, so everyone called him "Ears." The offer he made me was for kind of a dual scholarship: I'd play football for him and baseball for Toby Greene, the A&M coach at the time. Ears Whitworth would leave Oklahoma in '54 to become head coach at Alabama, his alma mater, where he had Bart Starr as a senior quarterback and still went 0-10. At A&M, he had a couple of pretty good years. He'd play a spread offense every once in a while, and although I was an end, he wanted to use me to pass in those situations, because he had scouted me in a game against Picher and saw that I could throw the ball a long way.

I signed a letter of intent to play football for Whitworth on February 23rd, 1953, not long after I'd turned 16, and he invited Mom and me to the campus. We saw Oklahoma A&M beat the St. Louis University Billikens in a double-overtime basketball game, 60-58. The famed coach Eddie Hickey was with the Billikens then, and the two teams had a great rivalry.

I remember being up there in Gallagher Hall, the basketball arena, and just looking the old place over. Man, I loved being there, and I would've loved to have gone to school at A&M and played Division One football. But, as it turned out, I did the right thing. I chose full-time baseball.

That summer, thankfully, my arm came back a little bit. I was fortunate that I didn't have a loss of velocity, but I think I would've been *really* fast if my football accident hadn't happened. As it was, I had to really learn how to pitch. Not only did I have to find better control, I also had to try to develop a breaking ball to go along with my fastball.

The St. Louis Cardinals were showing an active interest in me, so after my graduation from Chelsea High in May of '53, their organization set me up with a semipro team in Minden, Louisiana, called the Minden

953 ALL STAR BASEBALL H.S. PLAYED OK

BERNICE 1950
MINDEN 1951
MINDEN 1952
BIG EIGHT CHAMPS
MINDEN 1953

Redbirds, whose general manager was an old guy named T.C. Blossom. There was a regular league down there in the lumber country of northwest Louisiana, and a good restaurant in Minden where the ballplayers could eat free. I made a lot of friends down there that summer, traveling to play in little towns like Bastrop, Houma, Farmerville, and Ruston. Except for me, the whole Minden roster was made up of college players.

As had been the case with the Ban Johnson League, all the ballplayers got day jobs. Mine was delivering cases of pop for the Coca-Cola Bottling Company. I wore coveralls and rode a truck around to all the country stores in the parish, loading out those bottles in the old wooden cases. It was hot and muggy down in Louisiana, and the coveralls weren't exactly lightweight, so I ended up drinking a lot of Coke to cool off—so much that I got to where I couldn't stand the taste of it any more.

Then, one day, I met a guy who was delivering Grapette. He was sick of drinking Grapette, and I was sick of drinking Coke, so we switched out a bottle or two. I was just a swamper, an assistant to the old guy who drove the route, and he didn't approve, so he turned me in to the boss, Old Man Hunter, for drinking a Grapette on the job.

It wasn't long before the old man called me in to his office, where he sat with two cocker spaniels beside him.

"You're wearing our uniform," he said, "and that means you're out there working for Coca-Cola. You drink nothing but Coca-Cola. It's *good* for you."

At that point, he took a bottle of Coke and poured it into a cup, setting it on the floor in front of the dogs. I guess they were thirsty, because they lapped it right up.

"See?" he almost shouted at me. "Even dogs like it! It's *good* for 'em!"

Then he started really chewing my ass out, all because I'd drunk *one* stinking bottle of Grapette. I stood there and took it, getting madder and madder, until finally I'd had enough.

"Look," I said, interrupting his tirade, "I've had enough of this shit, and I don't have to hear any more of it. I was thirsty. I don't have to work for you. Someone else'll hire me, if that's what you want."

He'd really been on a roll, but he caught himself then.

"Well, all right," he said. "All right." And damned if he didn't take me off the truck and put me in the back of the plant, scraping off old Coca-Cola signs so they could be repainted. It was an easy job. It was cool back there.

So Old Man Hunter turned out to be an okay guy.

* * * *

Even though my daytime job had gotten easier, I'd gone to Minden to pitch, and I wasn't doing much of that. The team was full of older college players as well as some veterans, and I didn't have a lot of opportunity to show what I could do. There were a couple of pitchers in front of me—a good left-hander named Raymond Taliaferro, who'd spend some time in the Detroit minor league system, and a right-hander, Milford Andrews, who threw really well and would go on to be a star with Louisiana Tech. Those two ate up most of the mound time.

Once, a barnstorming team from Zwolle, Louisiana, came through for an exhibition game, and I got the nod, striking out 21 guys. I figured I'd made the best of the opportunity and I'd surely get more of a chance to pitch after that, but it didn't happen.

That summer, Galen Hudspeth was pitching for a Ban Johnson League team in Independence, Kansas, managed by an insurance man named Charlie Stewart. He happened to be a cousin of our English and speech teacher at Chelsea, Mrs. Floyd.

I called Galen from Louisiana and told him I wasn't getting any work with the Redbirds. He told Charlie Stewart I was looking for another team, and pretty quickly Charlie called up and told me, "Boy, we could use you up here." He promised me that if I'd come play for his team, he'd get me a summer job with Sinclair Oil, which had its headquarters in Independence. So I went to Kansas and worked during the day adding up the tickets on stripper-well production, an easy job that paid pretty well. Charlie also gave me $400 cash under the table.

I was there for a little over a month, and then Minden got into the playoffs at the end of the season, and the team wanted me to come back down to Louisiana. Some of the team members had left to go to college, so the playoff roster was a little thin.

I rejoined the Redbirds for the final game, and I was called in to relieve a pitcher I really liked named Benny McArdle, a left-hander who'd been a guard on the Louisiana State University basketball team with future NBA star Bob Pettit. I'd seen him play on that LSU team against the University of Tulsa, when Tulsa beat them by about 10 points.

When I came in to relieve McArdle, there was a man on third. I threw a pitch that came in on the fists of the batter, and he hit a little dribbler down the third-base line that drove in the winning run.

I've always said that I've never cried over losing a ballgame, but that's not quite true. I cried once. You might figure it would've been after the Mazeroski home run that won the 1960 World Series for the Pirates—but it wasn't. It was on that ball field down in Louisiana in 1953, when I wasn't able to save the game for McArdle and the rest of the team. I mean, I did the job. It was just one of those things. But that was the only time I ever shed a tear for something I did on the diamond. That day, I felt so bad for my teammates that I cried.

03

THE $100 PITCH

In the fall of '53, after I'd played for both the semipro team in Minden, Louisiana, and the Ban Johnson League team in Independence, Kansas, one of the most famous names in baseball flew my mother and me up to Pittsburgh so that he could work me out. As just about everybody knows, Branch Rickey was famous for signing Jackie Robinson to a minor league contract with the Brooklyn Dodgers organization back in 1945, which led to the breaking of the color barrier in Major League Baseball. When Mom and I met him, he was the Pittsburgh Pirates general manager.

The Pirates had a scout named Howie Haak, an old catcher, who had scouted me and recommended me for the Pirates. Rickey was interested enough to fly us in and put us up in the Schenley Hotel; you could look out the window of the room and see Forbes Field, home of the Pirates. That's where Rickey took me to see what I had. He got a catcher to warm me up, and I started throwing to him out in front of the first-base dugout. Since it was football season, the Pittsburgh Steelers were working out on the field, and Jimmy Finks—a friend of mine who'd played for the University of Tulsa before joining the Steelers as a quarterback and defensive back— saw me and came over.

"Ralph," he said, "what the hell are *you* doing here in the middle of November?"

I said, "Well, Jimmy, I'm trying out for the Pirates."

After I'd warmed up, Rickey walked out in front of the catcher and carefully set a hundred-dollar bill down on home plate. He looked over at me.

"Hit that bill," he told me, "and I'll give it to you."

Well, I'd never seen a hundred-dollar bill before. I threw at it and barely missed it.

"Would you give me one more chance?" I asked Rickey.

"All right," he said.

So I threw again—and *hit* it. He gave me the bill and took my mother and me back into his office. It was like a classic movie, the way he did it, sitting back in a corner, his face shaded, talking to my mom and me like a father. "We'll take care of him and see that he doesn't get the big-city disease, as we call it," he told her. "Do you go to church?" he asked me. He really put it on thick.

Finally, my mom got to the point. "Enough of all this," she told him. "What's your best offer?"

"Well," Rickey replied, "we'll give you $36,000—but it'll be spread over a six-year period."

I thought about that a minute. "You mean," I asked, "if I make the Pirates in my fifth or sixth year, I'll still be locked into this amount?"

"That's right. That's the deal."

I said, "If I make the big leagues, I think I'll have a chance to make a lot more money than that. Otherwise, I shouldn't even be trying to play ball for a living."

So we turned Branch Rickey down and went back home to Chelsea. It had been interesting to meet him, the guy who'd brought up Robinson and done so much more in baseball. He was a good guy with a job to do, and he did it well. But we knew I was being scouted by a lot of teams, and we figured we could get a better deal. Mom and I were the only ones making the decisions about my career; Dad had remarried and moved on.

As it turned out, I got *two* better deals—and that was something that made headlines all across the country, although the stories weren't always positive.

Here's how it happened: I was interested in both the New York Yankees and the St. Louis Cardinals, and they were both interested in me. Then, on November 19, 1953, I signed with the Yankees for $4,000. That was not a random amount. Owners had been spending so much money signing up prospects and giving big bonuses that Major League Baseball had passed a rule saying that any new player who signed for more than $4,000 had to be put on the 25-man major league roster. So a kid who got more than that amount for signing a contract—even though he wouldn't be ready for the big leagues and wouldn't be playing very much at that level, if at all—would have to take a roster spot that would otherwise belong to someone who could actually help the team. A few prospects still signed for more than $4,000 and were put on 25-man rosters, but because of that rule, most of us got offered $4,000 or less to sign.

Tom Greenwade, from Willard, Missouri, was the scout who signed me for the New York Yankees. He'd signed Mickey Mantle for $1,100 in the back seat of his car late one night, and he'd also helped sign Jackie Robinson, when he had scouted with the Dodgers before becoming part of the Yankees system. In those days, there was a popular TV commercial for Bardahl, a motor-oil additive, that featured a cartoon of a man in a black hat and black trenchcoat; Greenwade's nickname was "Blackie Bardahl," because he dressed all in black and drove a big black Cadillac. After pulling it up in front of our house in Chelsea on that November morning, he'd gotten out and come in to sign me, offering a $2,000 bonus and a $2,000 salary for '54, regardless of where I ended up in the minors. It sounded good to me, so I agreed.

"Here's what you do," he says. "Go down and send a telegram to the Yankees, agreeing to sign for those amounts, and then get your mother to sign it, since you're only seventeen."

So Mom and I went into Chelsea, sent the telegram, and came home. It was only an hour or two before another car pulled up outside our house and Freddie Hahn, the scout who'd first seen me pitch when I was 15 at the Cardinals' tryout camp in Pryor, and Ferrell Anderson got out. Ferrell Anderson was an ex-big-league catcher from Joplin who'd recently caught me in a game over in Cassville, Missouri. I pitched for the town team, and we were playing against a barnstorming team of pros, including a couple of big-leaguers—they used to play those town-team games until the snow flew. I shut the barnstormers out 3-0, and Cliff Mapes—the ex-Yankee who'd just finished his major league career—hit a homerun over the centerfield fence to win the game for me. I don't think those farmers had ever seen a ball hit like that.

Now here was Ferrell Anderson on our doorstep, and I know that Freddie Hahn had brought him to help seal a deal with me. When we all started talking about me signing with the Cardinals, Anderson said, "You'll start in Omaha, in A ball, and while we can't give you any more money than the Yankees can give you to sign, I'll catch you over there, and you'll probably win a dozen or 15 games."

I liked Ferrell Anderson. He was a good catcher and a good guy, and I thought it would be good to work with him at Omaha. So I said, "Well, here's what I've done. I just sent a telegram to the Yankees agreeing to their terms, and I don't know if I can get out of that."

"That doesn't mean a thing," Freddie Hahn told me. "Until they get your name on a contract, it's not binding."

I didn't know anything about contract deals, so I took his word for it. "Okay," I said, "I'll sign with you."

They just happened to have a contract with them, and I signed it, looking forward to playing with Ferrell Anderson at Omaha. But my anticipation was pretty short-lived. That evening, I got a call from the Associated Press office in Oklahoma City.

"What's going on?" the guy asked. "We saw that you'd signed with the Yankees, and then we see that you've signed with the Cardinals. Which one is it?"

I had no comment.

* * * *

Things blew up pretty quickly then. The story of my signing with two different teams made sports pages all over the country, and Ford Frick, the Commissioner of Major League Baseball, got involved. He sent a guy to Chelsea named Buck Green, who'd been with either the FBI or the CIA and was now a special investigator for Frick's office. He spent five days in town interviewing all these different people, including the CHS superintendent, checking up on my character. He visited the house and talked to my family members, and he turned out to be a really nice guy, a great guy.

So Buck Green made his report to the commissioner's office, and in early December, Frick handed down his decision. He said that since a cable wire was binding—despite what Freddie Hahn had told me—I was the property of the Yankees.

I didn't officially join the Yankees until just after my 18th birthday, when it became legal for me to sign the contract. That happened on January 9, 1954, and I believe I signed the next day. (Mom and I had known that I could've signed earlier if we could give evidence showing

I was a hardship case. We didn't have much money and maybe we could've done that, but we were too proud to pursue it.) At the time I was going to college at NEO in Miami; one of the newspaper people suggested that we drive over to Commerce, which was only four miles away, and see if we could find Mickey, who was spending the off-season at home after finishing his third year as a Yankee, and get

Mickey Mantle and Ralph Terry shake hands inside Billie's Pool Hall in Commerce, Oklahoma, just after Ralph had signed with the New York Yankees. The second photo was the one printed in newspapers.

a picture of the two of us—Yankee star and future Yankee, both out of northeastern Oklahoma.

Mickey was about five years older than me, so although the Chelsea and Commerce high school teams went head-to-head each year, I never played against him. By the time I got to the ninth grade at Chelsea and started playing high school ball, he'd already graduated. I did play against his twin brothers, Ray and Roy, who were a year behind me in school.

But even though he was older, I knew Mickey, and I knew where he hung out in Commerce. It was a classic pool hall, a real dive. Sure enough, we went in and there he was, shooting a game. But he stopped and congratulated me and agreed to be photographed. The shot has since become kind of famous, but there's something most people don't know about it. The picture everyone has seen, with Mickey and me shaking hands, has a blank wall in the background. But that's actually the *second* photo that was taken. The first one had a bunch of pool cues hanging behind us, and the photographer or reporter or someone thought that didn't look very wholesome, so they moved us to another wall.

The contract Mickey and I celebrated with that handshake was a special one because it started me with the big-league team. This was an important thing, because in those days when you signed with a team, you got three options. No matter what level you entered, from Class D to AAA, you had those three options, each one for a year.

Let's say you signed a contract with a double-A team. If you couldn't make it at that level, the parent team could option you to a team in a lower league. That could go on for three years. So at the end of that three-year period, if you couldn't stick on the double-A roster, you'd be released.

On the other hand, if you were good enough to move up a notch to triple-A, then you'd have three years of options with *that* team. If you made it to the big leagues, there were three *more* options. Really, a player that started at one of the lower levels could be controlled by the major league team forever, or at least for most or even all of his career.

The Yankees starting me at the big-league level meant that they only had a three-year total option on me. If I wasn't with the parent team at the end of those three years, I'd have to be cut loose; if that happened, I figured I'd have a pretty good chance of catching on with another big-league team—a lot better than if I'd signed at a lower level and then either gotten released or tied up for years. So a couple of months later, as a brand-new Yankee, I got on the train at the old Frisco Depot in downtown Tulsa, headed down through New Orleans, and changed trains in Jacksonville, Florida, for my final destination of St. Petersburg, Florida. It was the first journey I'd made as a pro ballplayer.

* * * *

Before going any further, I want to tell you a little more about my best friend and fellow ballplayer, Galen Hudspeth. Like me, he wanted to play baseball for a living, and even though our paths started taking us to different places and teams during the summer, we always found opportunities to get together.

The summer after we graduated from Chelsea, Tom Greenwade was also scouting Galen for the Yankees. I remember playing in a game with him late that summer, although I can't recall the team we were on. It may just have been a kind of exhibition team, put together to play the B.F. Goodrich company team out of Miami, Oklahoma. They were pretty good. Galen and I came out of Chelsea to play the games, so it must've been after the playoffs in Louisiana.

Galen was pitching, and he started slow. I don't remember who was catching him, but I *do* remember saying to the manager, "Hey, let me take over as catcher." I did, and once I got behind the plate, he

Tom Greenwade and Mickey Mantle sign a glove for a Holiday Inn employee in Joplin, Missouri.

straightened out and ended up striking out 15 or 18 guys. We just had an unspoken bond that stretched back to McIntosh grade school in Chelsea, and we had always worked well together on the diamond.

Greenwade was in the stands that night, and he signed Galen after seeing him pitch that game. Rechristened "Van" Hudspeth, which was his real first name, he made his pro debut in 1954 with the McAlester Rockets in the Class D Sooner State League, alongside Ray and Roy Mantle, Mickey's younger twin brothers. The team was tops in its league that year, and Galen was a workhorse, winning 15 games and losing 15, with a good ERA of 3.17. I think he was a little too *much* of a workhorse. He had a manager named Bunny Mick, a first baseman and outfielder who'd played in the Yankees system for years without making it to the majors, and Mick used Galen as both a starter and reliever. I think he wore Galen's arm out, because he never won another game in pro ball.

The next year, Galen moved up to Class C, going to the Monroe Sports in the Cotton State League, where he was 0-2 before being released by the Yankees. By that time, he was having arm trouble, and he never bounced back.

I've always thought that Galen might have made it as a hitter instead of a pitcher. His first year at McAlester, he hit .272 with a couple of home runs. He played first base well, and he had some power. But he took his shot as a pitcher, and he was able to compete in the minors as a Yankee farmhand for two years, which is more than most high school athletes, even the very good ones, will ever be able to say.

* * * *

I took the train to spring training in St. Petersburg in early 1954 with another pitcher, Jack Urban from Omaha, who'd later play for the Kansas City A's. We were joining a bunch of other hot prospects, maybe 50 of them, from the Yankees organization for a special, pre-spring training camp. There were good players from all levels, and I especially remember the catchers, Gus Triandos and Lou Berberet, and a couple of infielders who'd later be my Yankee teammates, Tony Kubek and Bobby Richardson.

One day we were having an intersquad game, and I was pitching with runners on first and third. They decided to pull a delayed double steal, which can be a beautiful play. When the pitcher goes into his stretch and looks at the guy on first, the guy on third takes off, and the minute the runner on first sees the man on third break for home, he jumps off the bag while the pitcher's still looking at him. Of course, the natural impulse for the pitcher is to throw to first base, because he's got the runner, but that allows the one on third to score. It's a play that's pulled a lot on rookies.

I was a rookie, but I knew something was up. So I went into my stretch, the guy on first jumped off, and I jumped off the mound and nailed the runner off third.

"Time out!" called Casey Stengel, who even then was a baseball legend. He walked out to the mound where I stood.

"Man," he said, "that was pretty sharp. Where'd you learn how to handle that play?"

I said, "Well, an old pitcher used to come around when I was in high school. He'd always tell me, 'Keep your cap pulled down, and don't worry about the guy on first—you've got all day to get him.'"

"What was his name?" Casey asked me.

"Ben Tincup. He was an Indian."

"Ben Tincup?" Casey said. "Hell, I played with *him*. He pitched for Louisville."

Before that, I'd just been a face in the crowd to him. But thanks to Ben Tincup and what he'd taught me, Casey started to notice me and what I was doing.

* * * *

I knew that once regular spring training started, the Yankees weren't going to keep me on the 25-man roster. I'd be on the 40-man roster, and they'd be sending me home for a month or so before I reported to Class-A Binghamton, New York, for the start of the Eastern League season.

So I went to Casey and made him an offer. "Look," I said, "if I go home, I'll just get out of shape, and I'm in pretty good shape now. Could I stay and just pitch batting practice? If I hang around, maybe I'll learn something."

He said, "That's a great idea," and told the general manager and the traveling secretary he wanted to keep me there for spring training, which meant I'd be going to Yankees camp at St. Petersburg, Florida, with the big-leaguers for three weeks.

One of those big-leaguers was Yogi Berra, who'd been a Yankee star since the late '40s. One day I was pitching batting practice to him, and for some reason he couldn't even hit it out of the cage—and Yogi could hit on Christmas day. He was a great fastball hitter.

So he shouts out at me, "Put something *on* the ball." I wasn't throwing hard enough for him.

Well, something like that can really get your Irish up, and he just really pissed me off. So I started *smoking* him. For about ten minutes, I stood there on the mound and threw him hard stuff, putting as much power behind it as I could. And he couldn't get on my fastballs. He still wasn't getting anything out of the cage. Finally, he just threw the bat down and walked away.

I once heard a guy say that modesty, once lost, is never regained. But I have to tell this story anyway, even though it's not only immodest but it also gets to me every time I think about it. One day, a bunch of writers were hanging around the batting cage, and Casey pointed to me and gave me the greatest compliment I've ever received. He said, "This is the finest pitching prospect I've laid eyes on since I've been in baseball."

"Christy Mathewson?" one of the writers asked.

"I mean, Ralph Terry is the best pitching prospect I've ever seen," Casey said again. "Watch how he fields his position." He told them all this stuff, and what he said about me got into the *Sporting News*. You can look it up.

* * * *

The spring-training camp for the Boston Red Sox was in Sarasota, and both the visitors and the Red Sox had their locker rooms in the same old frame building. If you were a member of the visiting team, you had to walk through their locker room to get to yours. So one day after a long stretch of throwing batting practice I came through, and there was Ted

Williams, sitting beside his locker. He was the only guy in there. I'd gone in to change my sweatshirt and get a drink, but I didn't know my way around very well.

"What do you need, kid?" he asked.

"I'm thirsty. I need a drink."

"Go over there in the corner and get yourself a Coke," he said. "Put it under my name."

They had a cheat sheet put up with the names of the players, and you put a mark by your name when you got a drink and settled up with the clubhouse guy later on.

I thanked him and got my Coke.

"Sit down, kid," he said.

I did.

"Where you from?"

"Oklahoma."

"Where are you gonna go this year?'"

"I think they're going to send me to the Eastern League."

So we talked, and I finished my drink, and it was just like that old TV commercial with Mean Joe Green, when the kid gives him a Coke—except that it was Ted Williams, the star athlete, buying the *kid* one, and the kid was me. He was a special man, and I started getting to know him that day, just because of his kindness to a rookie pitcher on his way to a season of A ball.

Pretty soon exhibition games started up, and Casey put me in one against the Washington Senators. Their star infielder Pete Runnels hit an opposite-field fly ball off me that went down the line for a double.

When I was in the dugout, I said to Casey, "That was kind of a fluke hit."

"Yeah," Casey said. "He hits everything that way."

We went on a spring training road trip, and one evening when we were in West Palm Beach to play the Philadelphia A's, Moose Skowron took me and a couple of other rookies out for pizza. I'd never had a pizza before. We didn't have a lot of Italians in Rogers County, Oklahoma.

Later on, the team traveled to Vero Beach to play the Brooklyn Dodgers, who were coming off their loss to the Yankees in the 1953 World Series. Bob Grim, an ex-Marine, started the game. He had a short-arm delivery and really smoked it in there. He also had a little slider. Boy, he was on top of things, and I wasn't surprised when he was voted American League Rookie of the Year at the end of the season.

That day, he pitched seven innings, and when he left, the Yankees were trailing 4-1. Then Casey put me in.

I faced four batters: Wally Moon, Duke Snider, Don Zimmer, and Don Hoak. Moon hit a fly ball to short right field. I got Snyder out with a fastball. He hit the highest popup I'd ever seen to our second baseman. Zimmer hit a ground ball to third base that Gil McDougald misplayed for an error. Hoak followed with another grounder to third, and McDougald threw him out.

I was 18 years old. And even though it was just spring training and I knew I was headed for minor league camp, it made me feel pretty good to be able to pitch a scoreless inning against the Yankees' biggest National League rivals.

* * * *

The Class A Eastern League had eight teams, four in Pennsylvania and four in New York. The Pennsylvania teams were located in Allentown, Reading, Williamsport, and Wilkes-Barre, the New York teams in Schenectady, Elmira, Albany, and Binghamton.

I started out slowly for the Binghamton Triplets—at one point, I was 3-7—and I knew something had to change. So I went to our manager Phil Page, who was an old left-handed relief pitcher, and I said, "I throw hard for five innings, but after that, my fastball isn't enough. Let me have a couple days off to rest and work on the curveball they taught me in spring training. I'm about to get it." As I said earlier, I knew I needed a curveball, especially after getting my shoulder hurt in high school, and I'd been fooling with one since then, but I didn't really have any confidence in it. The Yankees had shown me a different way of throwing it at that pre-spring training camp, and I was sure I could make it work if I spent enough time practicing.

He said okay, he wouldn't pitch me for a few days.

We went to Schenectady next, and a big red-headed right-hander, a bonus baby named Bob Bonebrake, was scheduled to pitch. I was running in the outfield during batting practice, expecting another day off, when the batboy came out and flagged me down.

"You've got to warm up," he said. "Bonebrake's arm is bothering him, so you've got to pitch."

The Schenectady Blue Jays were a Philadelphia Phillies farm club, and one of their future stars, Dick "Turk" Farrell, was on the mound that day. He was a hell of a pitcher, but we beat them 1-0. Bobby Richardson hit a triple for us and scored on a sacrifice fly, while I pitched a one-hitter.

That was the turning point for me. The curve started working, going along with my fastball, and I went eight out of my last 10 to finish 11-9 with a 3.30 ERA. My final game of the season I lost 3-2 in ten innings. I ended up with 12 complete games, 120 strikeouts, and 64 walks.

It was while I was at Binghamton that I had one of my most memorable baseball experiences. At about the middle of the season, the Yankees and the Cincinnati Reds met at Cooperstown on an off-day to play an exhibition game, with proceeds going to the National Baseball Hall of Fame Museum. Binghamton was only about an hour's drive from Cooperstown, so I went down there to Abner Doubleday Field to watch.

Two of the all-time greats Ralph visited with on that long-ago day at Doubleday Field: Denton True "Cy" Young (left), who still holds the big-league record for wins with 511, and Tyrus Raymond "Ty" Cobb (above), all-time leader in career batting average (.366 or .367 –sources differ). Both played 22 seasons in the majors.

Doubleday Field was a small park that could hold maybe 10,000, but for this game they had temporary bleachers out in front of the fences. If you hit a ball into those bleachers, it was an automatic double. They were full. The whole stadium was packed. I wandered down to the third-base dugout, where the Yankees were, and got Jim Turner's attention. He was the pitching coach, and he knew me from spring training.

"Let this kid in," Turner told the cop who was guarding the dugout. "This is an exhibition game, not a league game, so it's okay for him to sit on the bench."

The cop let me in, pointing down to the end of the dugout. "You can go down there and sit with those three old-timers," he said.

I made my way to the spot he'd indicated and sat down, with two of the old men in the corner of the dugout on my left, and the other one, who was holding a cane, on my right. I couldn't help but notice that he was wearing a World Series ring. When the second inning came around, I thought, "You know, I really ought to say hello and introduce myself," so I stuck out my hand to the old guy on the right and said, "Hi. Ralph Terry's my name. I'm a *pitcher*. Binghamton. Class A. Eastern League."

"Well, hello, Ralph," he said, shaking hands. "I'm Cy Young." Then he turned toward the other two.

"Shake hands with Zack Wheat," he said, and I said hello to that old Dodger slugger who'd be a Hall of Famer himself a few years later.

"And," added Cy Young, "this is Ty Cobb."

Ty Cobb? Tyrus Raymond Cobb? I was like, "Put her *there*, baby!"

I sat with them the whole game, listening to Cobb and Wheat talk hitting. Actually, Cobb was doing all the talking. He was very dogmatic and assertive: "This is the way you hit to the opposite field. This is the way you deaden the ball—you've got to pull your hands off the bat." Cy Young was the nicest old guy you'd ever want to meet. He'd grown up in a farming community in Ohio, and we talked about farming and fishing and pitching for the whole game.

I found out later he was 87 at the time. He died the next year.

It was a great day. I only have one regret about it. That whole time the four of us sat together talking and watching the Yankees and Reds play their fundraising game, I never asked any of those legendary old ballplayers for their autographs.

04

THE PATH TO THE BIG APPLE

When I started in pro ball, the minor league seasons were shorter than they are now, so when I was finished at Binghamton, I returned to NEO in Miami, starting a pattern of going to school in the off-season that would last for years. I never actually got a degree, but I sure compiled a lot of college hours from several different institutions.

I'd been a pretty good basketball player back at Chelsea, and that second year I played for NEO and its famous coach Red Robertson to help keep me in shape for baseball. I averaged 22 points a game, and I guess that was pretty good, since the school recently put me in its basketball hall of fame.

Then it was back to spring training. I was 19 years old, coming off a good year at Binghamton, and I had a great spring—so good that I thought I was going to make the big leagues right out of camp. The last day before we broke to go north, I pitched against the Phillies, who had a great ballclub then. Robin Roberts, their ace, was pitching against us, and we locked up for six innings, nothing to nothing.

When I got to the dugout after my part of the sixth, Jim Turner, our pitching coach, was waiting for me. "What do you think?" he asked. "Do you want to go to the seventh?"

"Sure," I told him.

In those days, you didn't really pitch yourself *onto* the parent club—you pitched yourself *off.* And you did that by making mistakes.

Maybe I made a mistake going out for the seventh inning. Maybe not. But the first thing I did was walk Richie Ashburn, their future Hall of Famer and the fastest guy on the team. Bobby Morgan, the Phillies' second baseman, came up after that. They had the hit and run on, and I threw one high and inside that he managed to bloop down the right field line. Ashburn scored standing up, and it was a 1-0 game. Even though I'd allowed that single run, I figured I'd pitched a hell of a game against Robbie, who was then the best right-hander in the National League.

So I was confident that I'd made the ballclub. Then Bill McCorry, the Yankees' traveling secretary, bolstered my confidence further. All the teams used those old Priesmeyer trunks, big and rectangular and really solid, to carry the players' belongings, and McCorry called me over and gave me the tickets I needed to put on my trunk for the train trip to New York City.

What else did I need to tell me I was a New York Yankee? That's what I *thought*, anyway.

The team was staying at the Serena Hotel in St. Petersburg. The morning of the day we were to leave for New York, I went downstairs for breakfast, and Casey Stengel was in the lobby with his newspaper, waiting for me.

"Sit down, kid," he said, and I knew I wasn't getting good news.

I sat down.

"Kid," he began, "you had a great spring, but I've got to send you out to Denver. I've got the same pitching staff I had last year, and when we go north, we'll have a lot of rainouts and off-days, and I can get by with three starters for the first month or so.

"Whenever I *did* need you, you might not be in shape to pitch, because you hadn't been in any games. I already know what you can do, so

I'm going to send you out to Denver, where you'll start regular. That way, you'll stay in shape, and if I need you, I can call you up and you'll be ready."

Sure, I was disappointed. But I loved Stengel, and for us players, he was God. Whatever he said went.

So I started the 1955 season in Denver, which was the Yankees' new Triple-A affiliate in the American Association. Before that year, I would've been going to the Kansas City Blues, the Yankees' Triple-A club in the American Association. But there'd been a shakeup after the 1954 season. The American League Philadelphia A's had moved to Kansas City, and the Blues had moved to Denver and become the Bears.

The Bears were managed by Ralph Houk, a backup catcher and future Yankees manager who'd ended his playing career with the Yankees in 1954 (although he'd appear in 15 games with the '55 Bears as a player). Don Larsen, acquired by the Yankees in late '54 via a big 17-player trade with the Orioles that also brought Bob Turley to New York, was another member of the Bears pitching staff, sent there by the parent club to get into shape. He'd be called up later in the season.

A note here about that Orioles-Yankees deal: During my years as a professional ballplayer, there were two trades that I think really shot the New York Yankees ahead of their American League competition. One was the swap that got us Roger Maris in 1959, which I'll talk about a little later. The other was that 1954 blockbuster, which brought Larsen and Turley to the team. Engineered by Yankees general manager George Weiss and Orioles GM Paul Richards, it was the biggest trade in major league history at that time. The Orioles sent eight men—pitchers Turley, Larsen, and Mike Blyzka; Billy Hunter, their starting shortstop; catcher Darrell Johnson; first baseman Dick Kryhoski; and outfielders Jim Fridley and Ted del Guercio (a minor leaguer)—to the Yankees. In return, the Yankees gave them nine guys—pitchers Harry Byrd, Jim McDonald, and Bill Miller; minor league infielders Don Leppert and Kal

Segrist; shortstop Willy Miranda; outfielder Gene Woodling (a future Baltimore star); and a pair of Triple-A catchers who'd both go on to have good major league careers, Gus Triandos and Hal Smith. Smith had just won the 1954 American Association batting title with Columbus, the St. Louis Cardinals' Triple-A affiliate.

While this was bigger than any other deal ever made between a pair of big-league clubs, it was in many ways exactly the kind of trade the Yankees made with teams like Baltimore and, later, the Kansas City A's. These were cellar teams, second-division, and they'd often have a half-dozen positions they needed to fill, while the Yankees were just trying to get stronger in a specific area or two. In these situations, New York GM Weiss would typically give up several players to get the one or two guys he wanted.

A couple of the other players the Orioles swapped, especially Billy Hunter, would help the Yankees a little, but the main Yankee acquisitions were the two big right-handers. Turley had been the ace of the Orioles staff in '54, going 14-15 (for a team that lost 100 games) while striking out 185, tying with the National League's Robin Roberts—my foe in the final spring training game of '55—for most strikeouts in the majors. However, he'd also led the major leagues in walks with 181. Larsen had lost more games during the '54 season than any other pitcher in either league, going 3-21 with the Orioles. But, like Turley, he was a hard thrower just starting his career in the majors.

One of the first things they both did once they got to the Yankees was shorten their deliveries. Both of them had been pitching from full windups, and during a full windup a sharp opposing coach or player could see how a pitcher's hand was turned, whether he was poised to throw a fastball or a curve, and signal the batter about what was coming. I think that's what was happening with both those guys—they were tipping their pitches. You find out things like that when you get traded, because the guys who used to be your opponents let you in on how they tried to get the advantage against you. So Larsen and Turley started hiding the ball in their gloves—something *all* pitchers do now—getting the sign, and just rocking and firing. They were big guys, and they didn't need big windups. So they shortened up and, boom, all of a sudden they were great.

That's *my* opinion, anyway. Whatever the reasons for their success as Yankees, they both would have a big effect on our ball club.

* * * *

I started out my 1955 American Association season going 7-5, and while I couldn't get my curve to break as well in Denver because of the high altitude and my ERA wasn't where I wanted it to be, I still had a winning record on a losing team. So I was a little surprised when Houk called me in after a home game in July and said, "Go get your suitcase. You're being sent down to Birmingham. You'll join 'em in Memphis. You've got a one o'clock flight."

They were sending me to the Birmingham Barons, the Yankees' Double-A affiliate in the Southern League.

This happened just about the time the Denver Bears had started to turn things around. We still had a losing record, but the team was heading upward. Besides Larsen, who'd go 9-1 before being called up to the parent club, we had Bobby Richardson, Tony Kubek, Marvelous Marv Throneberry, Woodie Held, and catcher Darrell Johnson, picked up in that trade with the Orioles, who'd go on to hit over .300 that year. It looked as though we might be good enough to get into the American Association playoffs.

"All right," I told Houk, "but I've been a part of this team. If they make the playoffs, I want a share of the money, whether it's the winner's or the loser's share, because I helped them get there."

"You have my word of honor as your manager," he said.

"And," I added, "If I'm going good down there, better than anyone else on the pitching staff, and you need to call a pitcher up, I want to be the guy."

"You bet," he said.

So I joined Birmingham for a series with the Memphis Chicks, a White Sox affiliate and a good ballclub. Luis Aparicio was their shortstop; he'd jump to the majors the next year and begin his Hall of Fame career. I pitched in that series and lost, 4-3. After that, though, I won seven in a row. At the end of that string, I had a 7-1 record and an ERA of 1.35—and when the Bears needed a pitcher, they called up a left-hander, Jim Kite, who was 7-7 for the Barons.

Ralph Houk was a very competitive guy, and I'm sure he had his reasons for bringing Kite instead of me to Denver. But for the first time in my professional baseball career, I felt betrayed and disillusioned. I not only lost heart, I lost my next three games, ending the season at Birmingham at 7-4 with a 3.35 ERA.

* * * *

The next spring, in 1956, marked my third year in the Yankee system. I went to spring training and got shipped out to Denver again, although I knew, because of the terms of my contract, I would probably see some time with the big club before the season was over.

Casey told me basically the same thing he'd said in '55, and I understood. Not only did he have his strong starting rotation returning from the year before; he also had a new veteran presence on his pitching staff. Over the winter, General Manager Weiss had traded five players, including a young minor leaguer named Whitey Herzog, to perennial cellar-dwellers the Washington Senators, getting shortstop Bobby Kline and

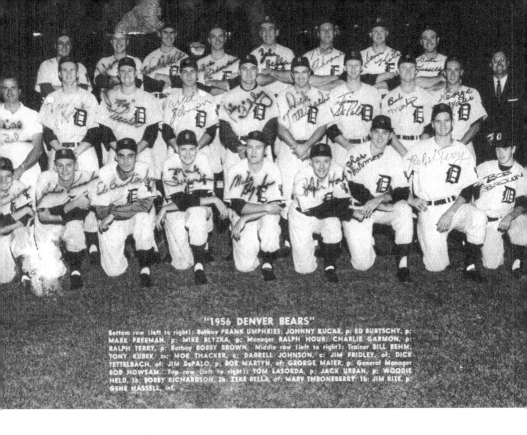

pitcher Mickey McDermott in return. After hitting .221 in 140 at-bats for the 1955 Senators, Kline would never play in the majors again, but that didn't matter much to Weiss. McDermott was the guy he wanted. A lefty, McDermott had won 18 games for the Red Sox in '53 and just gone 10-10 for the last-place Senators, who'd finished a dismal 53-101 in 1955. The New York Times sports columnist Arthur Daley called McDermott "pennant insurance." As far as I was concerned, he just helped insure that I started the season in the minors.

While I had been pitching for Birmingham the year before, the Bears had made it to the first round of the American Association playoffs, getting swept by the Minneapolis Millers 4-0. As I'd told Houk back when I was sent down, I wanted my share of the first-round money, which was $300—a lot of cash then. So after reporting to the Bears for the beginning of the '55 season, I asked him about it.

"Well," he said, "I couldn't do anything. The players decided. They took a vote, and they voted against giving you a share, since you hadn't been here the whole season."

"But you gave me your word," I said. "And you sat in when they voted."

"I couldn't do anything," he said again. "It was the players."

I knew he was telling the truth when he said managers couldn't vote. But I also knew that they could stand up in those meetings and speak on behalf of their players. Later on, when I was a part of Yankees teams that won World Series titles, we always gave something to the guys who'd been with us only part of a season.

But I got nothing from the Bears, and that was the end of that.

Although 1956 was the season I was first called up to the Yankees, it was also a disillusioning year in some ways, especially when it came to my paychecks. On August 1, the Yankees flew me in from Wichita, where the Bears were playing a series, and put me on their roster, taking the place of Irv Noren, a left-handed outfielder and first baseman who'd hurt his knee. At the time, my record with Denver was 11-1. I was making $4,800 or $5,000 at Denver that year, and when you went up to the big leagues the minimum was $6,000. So I was up for a month, getting paid at that level, before the team sent me back down to Denver. When I got my first check from the Bears, I saw that I was being paid at my former, minor league rate, which was wrong. Contractually, it was very clear: Once you'd been called up, your major league contract superseded any others.

That fact, however, didn't seem to matter to Bob and Lee Howsam, the brothers who owned the Bears, or Yankees management, either. I pointed out what was going on, but my minor league paycheck didn't change.

We were in West Virginia toward the end of the season, playing the Charleston Senators, a Detroit Tigers farm club, when Lee McPhail came by. McPhail was the Yankees farm director at the time, and I figured he was the guy I needed to talk to about my salary discrepancy. So I flagged him down.

"The owners are paying me the minor league rate," I told him. "How come? Shouldn't I be getting paid the major league minimum?"

"Hmmm," he said. "Tell you what. I'll see you when the team gets to Minneapolis in a couple of weeks, and we'll get it straightened out, all right?"

"Sure. Thanks."

After the Charleston series, we were gathering at the airport when I saw Houk. "Hey," I said, "when are we going to see McPhail again?"

"Oh, we won't see him until after the season's over," said Houk.

We finished the regular season and the playoffs began. Starting for Denver in the first round, I beat the Omaha Cardinals, and we eventually advanced to the finals. The checks were coming in for my teammates, but not for me. It turned out that I wasn't going to be paid for being in the playoffs. The reason given was that my contract was for the *season*, while the other guys were getting paid by the *month*.

That pretty much did it for me. I stormed into Houk's office and said, "Look, I quit. I'm going home to Chelsea. The hell with it."

"Listen, Ralph," he said, laying a guilt trip on me, "all these players, they've got families, they need the money. If you leave now, you'll be letting them down."

I guess I was a sucker for a sob story, because I stayed, even though by my count I'd been financially screwed three times in one season.

I only won one game as a Yankee in 1956. It was the one I wrote about in the introduction to this book, my first game in the big leagues, against the Red Sox at Fenway in August. As the starter, I went five and two-thirds innings, allowing three runs, striking out four, and walking three. Relief specialist Tom Morgan pitched a scoreless inning after me, and lefty Tommy Byrne finished up. The final score was 4-3. It was only the fourth loss for their ace, Tommy Brewer, who was 15-3 going into the game on the way to his best year in the bigs. He'd finish with 19 wins and 9 losses.

The two biggest back-to-back crowds ever in Fenway came in for that two-game series. In the second game, played the next day, Don Larsen hooked up with Willard Nixon, a pretty good pitcher with a reputation as a Yankee killer. For 10 innings, neither allowed a run. In the top of the 11th, with two outs, Mantle hit a pop fly to the corner of left field. The wind was swirling around out there and I could see from the bullpen that Ted Williams was really having trouble with the ball. He got to it, but it popped out of his mitt for an error. Mickey ended up on second base. From the stands, it looked like he'd muffed an easy play, and the crowd really got on him, booing the hell out of him. The very next pitch, Yogi hit a ball to left center, just in front of the little scoreboard on the Green Monster, and Williams made a beautiful running one-handed catch in the webbing of his glove for the final out. The fans in the stands gave him one of the greatest ovations I've ever heard; I don't know how much of it was motivated by guilt.

We went to the bottom of the eleventh, and Larsen got into trouble. With the bases loaded, two outs, and Williams at the plate, Casey called on Tommy Byrne again, giving him a lefty-lefty matchup.

Byrne went to three and two on Williams and then threw him a curve that looked pretty good from where I stood. The plate umpire called it ball four.

That forced in the winning run. And Williams, who was 0-3 that day, didn't even go to first base. He turned and flipped his bat about 50 feet straight up in the air, spinning it like a baton. It was unbelievable. Then he turned toward the press box, spit at it, and shot the crowd the bird. Afterwards, he was unrepentant.

"I'd spit again at the same people who [booed] me today," he told *Boston Globe* sportswriter Bob Holbrook.

Tom Yawkey, the Red Sox owner, fined him $5,000—and the fans took up a collection to pay his fine!

* * * *

I got two more starts for the Yankees in '56. The next one was against the Baltimore Orioles, a second-division ballclub, at home in Yankee Stadium. I figured, "Well, this ought to be easy"—and they beat me 10-5. Mantle hit his 40th homer in that one. A few days later, I started against the Orioles again in Baltimore's Memorial Stadium and lost 6-4. So I was 1-2 when they sent me back down to Denver, but I could take some pride in knowing that one win was in a big game that had snapped the Yankees' losing streak.

I'd only been up about a month, staying in the Commodore Hotel on Lexington Avenue when we weren't on the road. It was right downtown, and I remember walking around Broadway, taking in the sights. Once I went to a little downstairs walk-in place called Birdland. It was in the afternoon, and there were maybe five people in the whole place, listening to this blind black piano player—Ray Charles. *Damn Yankees*, the baseball musical, was big on Broadway at the time, and all the Yankees players got free tickets. Since it didn't cost me anything and I didn't have much else to do, I saw it four times. To this day, I can close my eyes and see Gwen Verdon singing "Whatever Lola Wants, Lola Gets."

The Yankees won the World Series that year, four games to three, against the Brooklyn Dodgers. I would've been eligible to play in the Series, but instead of calling me back up, they reacquired outfielder Enos Slaughter, who was in the final few years of his Hall of Fame career.

They needed a left-handed bat in the series, so they claimed him off waivers from Kansas City (releasing another famous player, 13-year Yankees shortstop Phil Rizzuto, to make room on the roster). The move paid off: Slaughter hit .350 in the Series, including a three-run homer that won the third game.

Although I'd had my problems with being shorted in the minors, the big-league team came through for me. Because I'd been a Yankee for a few weeks and won a game with the team, the players voted me a quarter-share of their series money, which came to $2,400. I took it and bought a '49 Ford and a shotgun, and used the rest to pay for a semester of college at Southwest Missouri State in Springfield that winter.

* * * *

I don't want to leave the 1956 season without saying something about one of the most famous games in World Series history. Baseball fans know that was game five, with Don Larsen pitching against the Dodgers' Sal "The Barber" Maglie. Maglie pitched a great complete game, allowing only five hits and two runs. Under normal circumstances, that would have been good enough to win. His mound opponent, though, did something that hasn't been done before or since. He threw a perfect game in the World Series.

I saw it all from a room at Burge Hospital in Springfield, where I was recovering from a tonsillectomy the team had pressured me to get in the off-season. I was 20 years old, weighed only about 170 pounds, and I was prone to getting tonsillitis and other throat problems. Management figured that if I had my tonsils removed I'd gain some weight, so I agreed, even though I wasn't really keen on having it done.

My roommate at the hospital was a kid who'd been stricken with polio. He was in an iron lung, flat on his back, and I fixed the TV so he could watch it in a mirror that was set up over his head. Together, we saw every pitch of that unprecedented feat, and when it was over, neither one of us could've been any prouder of Don Larsen, my ex-teammate on the Denver Bears who was now another shining star in the Yankee heavens.

05

TRADES—PART OF THE GAME

Nineteen fifty-seven was the year I finally stuck in the big leagues, although a major surprise awaited me that season.

Actually, there were two surprises. The first one came when I was in spring training. I got my first check, and I found out that the club had deducted $400, which had been the cost of my tonsillectomy and hospital stay. The Yankees had paid for everything; at no time had anyone with the club told me they wanted to be reimbursed.

Once again, I was faced with a financial situation I didn't think was right. So I went in to see Stengel.

"Look, Casey," I said, "here's what happened. I didn't want that operation, but I did it because they asked me to, and now they're taking it out of my salary. You know, Mickey Mantle's brother Roy had an operation, and they set him up for everything, first class. The bill came to $3,000, and they paid it—and Roy's a minor leaguer in Class C ball. It's not that they took care of *him*, because that's what they should've done. It's that they didn't take care of *me*."

Casey got right on the phone, and pretty soon the team's comptroller, Aaron Lanier, showed up.

"Take care of this kid," Casey told him after describing my problem. "Get his check straightened out. This is not right."

One of the many reasons I love Casey Stengel so much is that he went to bat for me and fixed that problem. I not only really appreciated that, I never forgot it.

I never forgot how tight the money guys on the club could be, either. There was a pitcher on the team in the early '50s named Bill "Hooks" Miller, a left-hander, making the minimum. Whenever you went on a road trip in those days, you wore a sports jacket and a tie, but Miller would never dress up.

So George Weiss called him in one day.

"Miller," he commanded, "dress like a Yankee!"

"Okay," Miller returned, "then *pay* me like a Yankee!"

* * * *

I made the team out of spring training, but I wasn't getting to pitch much. The Yankees were overflowing with pitching talent that year: Whitey Ford, Johnny Kucks, Don Larsen, and my roommate Tom Sturdivant started the first four games of the season, with Bob Turley, Art Ditmar, and Bobby Shantz waiting their turns. (The Yankees had gotten Shantz and Ditmar in a big trade with the Kansas City A's a couple of months earlier; "pennant insurance" Mickey McDermott, after a 2-6 season, had gone to Kansas City. New York would also pick up the team's future third baseman and former Ban Johnson League star Clete Boyer in June as the "player to be named later" in that deal.)

I saw a lot of great pitchers work during those first couple of months. But I also saw a horrific thing happen to one of them. If you're a baseball fan, you probably know about the incident.

On May 7, we were on the road, playing the Indians in Cleveland's Municipal Stadium. In the first inning, Herb Score—the 1955 Rookie of the

Year and an All-Star in both '55 and '56—had gotten leadoff hitter Hank Bauer on a groundout to third and was facing the second batter in our lineup, Gil McDougald. Gil was a real good fastball hitter, and after getting two quick strikes on him, Score threw him three curveballs that missed. I was in the dugout standing next to our pitching coach, Jim Turner, and we both knew Herb was going to come in with a fastball because he didn't want to walk McDougald and have to face Mantle, who'd won the Triple Crown the year before and was the most feared hitter in the game.

So Score threw a fastball, keeping it out and away from McDougald, and Gil hit a line drive right at Score. He never even saw it coming. It hit him in the left eye and blood just exploded. He reached up once and slapped his face, and then he hit the ground, kicking like a poleaxed steer.

"Oh, my God," Turner said. "He's dead."

The ball ricocheted so hard off Score's eye socket that third baseman Al Smith had plenty of time to throw McDougald out, but Gil only took three or four steps out of the batter's box toward first and then ran right to the mound. So did Smith. I heard, over the PA system, the announcer asking if there was a doctor in the house, and within moments there must've been a dozen doctors jumping that little low railing around home plate and heading out to the mound. They finally got Score up and walked him off. I was astounded that they didn't need a stretcher.

McDougald had been working on hitting the ball up the middle instead of pulling out too quickly on a curveball, and what a lot of people don't know or remember is that just about a week earlier, on May 1, he'd knocked pitcher Frank Lary out of the game with a shot to the kneecap. It was the top of the fourth, Lary had two outs on us, and Gil nailed him. Lary hobbled over, threw him out, and collapsed. Jim Bunning had to come out in relief at the top of the fifth.

Herb Score's condition was a lot more serious than Lary's, but he was able to come back from it, even though he was never the same pitcher. I think he was on his way to a Sandy Koufax kind of career before that happened. Later on he became an announcer for the team, and when I was with Cleveland, we played some golf together. He was a really great guy.

Neither Sturdivant, who was starting for us that day, nor I used protective cups when we pitched. After watching the ball hit Score with such frightening force that day, we both changed our minds and wore cups for the rest of our careers.

* * * *

I started for the first time on June 2, pitching the second game of a doubleheader against the Orioles and ending up with a complete-game, three-hit shutout. By the middle of June, I was 1-1 with a 3.05 ERA, having started two games and appeared in five others.

On the eighth of June, we were in Detroit, where I'd started and lost against the Tigers. I was in my hotel room getting into bed. The covers were really tight, and I caught my knee on them and slipped it out of place.

That knee had been hurt years before, when I was a sophomore, playing right end for the Chelsea Green Dragons against the team from Wyandotte High School. Wyandotte called a reverse, and this guy came in right in front of the ref and hit me with a crack-back block. Even though it was a blatant foul, the ref never threw his flag. It was a big rivalry and I got back in the game, playing the second half with my knee all taped up.

It took a while, but I healed, and it never really bothered me. Once in a while it'd catch on me, and I'd have to jiggle it until it slipped back in, but it never was a problem while I was playing ball.

Flash forward to that night in the Detroit hotel. I jiggled it and jiggled it, but I couldn't get it to slip back in. So I called the Yankees trainer, Gus Mauch. He came in, checked it out, and popped it right back.

Then along came the second surprise.

At the time there were rumors going around that someone was going to get traded at or before the June 15th deadline. Some said it was going to be pitcher Al Cicotte, a rookie who'd kicked around in the minors for eight years before getting the call. I'd heard it might even be me. I have no doubt that the people in charge of the team made up their minds the night Gus Mauch came down and took care of my knee. When anything like that happened—bingo—a trainer would go right straight to his manager. I'm sure that's why I became expendable. I might be damaged goods.

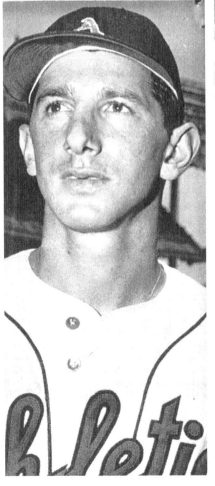

KANSAS CITY ATHLETICS
Ralph Terry (above) and Billy Martin (left)

June 15, 1957, was a Saturday. It was also the trade deadline. After Detroit, we'd played a three-game series at Chicago and then headed to Kansas City. After our game with the A's that day, Casey called me into his office. I knew what was coming. Before the game, he'd had me pitch all 45 minutes of batting practice. That was the kiss of death. He used me up so I wouldn't be coming back across the field the next day and beating his team.

"Well," he said, not looking up, "we just made a little trade."

"Who's involved?" I asked.

"You and Martin are going to Kansas City for Suitcase Simpson, Jim Pisoni, and Ryne Duren." At the time, Duren, a wild, hard thrower with some potential, was starting for the A's, but the guy they were after most was outfielder Harry "Suitcase" Simpson (whose nickname came from a character in the old *Toonerville Trolley* comic strip, not, as a lot of people think, because he was traded so many times). Although the Yankees still had Slaughter, they felt they needed another left-handed hitter on the roster.

(The Yankees also sent three minor leaguers to KC in the deal: outfielder Bob Martyn, second baseman Milt Graff, and infielder-outfielder Woodie Held, who'd go on to have a nice career in the big leagues, mostly with the Cleveland Indians.)

Casey looked at me. "I didn't make this trade, kid," he said. "Weiss made this trade."

"It sure seems like he gave up a hell of a lot more than he got."

"Yeah," Casey said. "That Martin's a hell of a player."

When you think about it, that was a pretty amusing thing to say to me under those circumstances.

"Look," he added, "you'll go over there and pitch regular, and you'll learn how to pitch in a small ballpark."

"Well, Casey…" I started.

"What?"

"I'm going to be out to beat your ass."

Billy Martin felt the same way. The day after the trade, he started at second base for Kansas City against the Yankees and had two hits, including a homer, scoring three times. It wasn't enough, though. Our former team won, 8-6.

I got my own chance a few days later. The A's went on the road, and I shut out the Senators, 2-0, with Virgil Trucks coming in and getting the last out. From there we went to New York, and on a Sunday afternoon, June 30, I pitched the second game of a doubleheader against Tom Sturdivant. I had two men out in the first with Mantle up. On a 3-2 count, I threw him a beautiful curve over the outside corner, a gorgeous strike and no mistake about it.

"Ball four," called the umpire.

They never had another baserunner until the eighth inning with two men out. I guess that's when I just ran out of gas. Norm Siebern got a single. Gil McDougald followed with a double to left center, scoring Siebern. Then Suitcase Simpson, playing right field that day, got a double off the Yankee Stadium scoreboard. He was a straightaway hitter, and my outfielders had been playing him to pull. They should've been playing him straight and playing McDougald to pull, too. I'd tried to position them, but they hadn't quite gotten the message.

I finished the game, losing 2-1. As far as I'm concerned, it should've been a perfect game until Siebern got his hit with two out in the eighth.

The next time I faced the Yankees was much later in the season, on August 30, when I matched up with Bob Turley, who'd win the American League Cy Young Award the next year. I threw a six-hitter and beat him 1-0 at Municipal Stadium in Kansas City. For the entire 1957 season, White Sox ace Early Wynn and I were the only two pitchers to shut out New York.

* * * *

Although I hated being traded from the Yankees, it didn't hit me nearly as hard as it did Billy Martin. When he got the news, he burst out crying. He was devastated.

"It's that first time getting traded," he told me. "And getting traded from the *Yankees.*" He'd broken in with New York in 1950, and except for a year off to fulfill his military service obligation, he'd been a Yankee ever since.

Billy was a good guy and a good friend. When Martin was on your team, it was *fun*, like playing sandlot ball when you were a kid. He could make three or four errors in a game and you'd still want him by your side. He was kind of morally bankrupt, but he was a wonderful competitor and a scrapper—he'd been in a lot of fights, and he hadn't won 'em all. His nose was pretty beat up. And he was an agitator, always needling the opposition.

One day in '56, Ted Williams grounded out, rounded first, and came back by our dugout. It was the middle of September, and we had the pennant sewed up, with the Red Sox way back in our rearview mirror. And as Williams passed by, Billy stood up on the dugout steps and yelled at him.

Boy," he shouted "wish I could go trout fishing and deer hunting after the season too, but we've got to play in that damn fall classic!"

"Go to hell, you little bastard," Williams grumbled back.

Although Martin had broken in a year before Mantle, Mickey was kind of his role model. In those days, when Mickey struck out, he'd come in the dugout, toss his batting helmet, throw the bat at the rack, kick the water cooler. Sometimes he'd even go up the runway from the dugout and kick out a light. He *hated* striking out.

Billy started doing the same thing after whiffing, not even realizing he was imitating Mickey. He'd throw the bat in the rack the same way, kick the water cooler, say the same cuss words.

Finally, Stengel called a clubhouse meeting.

"Look," he told Billy and Mickey, talking to them like they were little kids, "it's getting to where it's not safe in the dugout when you guys strike out. You've got to learn to take it. Bite your lip. Better yet, just laugh it off."

A couple of days later, we were playing Washington. They had a big left-hander whose name escapes me now, but one of his best pitches was a big, slow curveball. Billy batted before Mickey, and he struck out and came back to the dugout raising hell. Then Mickey, who was a sucker for a slow curve, struck out, and *he* came back and raised hell. A couple of innings later, Billy struck out again, and this time, he came into the dugout and laid down on the floor and started rolling around and laughing, saying stuff like, "The dirty SOB got me again." After whiffing a second time himself, Mickey joined Billy on the clubhouse floor.

"Ha ha," Mickey said. "He got me again on that old slow curve."

Casey let it go for a while, but he finally had enough. "All right," he told them. "You made your point. Now knock that shit off!"

* * * *

Even though Martin took the trade hard, I think he knew it was coming. He'd gotten a reputation as a bad influence on Mantle and, by inference, on the whole club, even though Mantle had won the Triple Crown in 1956 with 52 homers, 130 RBIs, and a .353 batting average. It didn't look to me like he'd hurt Mickey at all. Sometimes a club traded someone, and then management made up a story to justify the deal to the fans. In this case, the Yankees had Bobby Richardson coming up from the minors, which probably had a lot to do with their getting rid of Martin.

But to be fair, there *was* the Copacabana incident.

It happened on May 17, 1957, when Billy and Mickey, along with Yogi Berra, Whitey Ford, Hank Bauer, and Johnny Kucks—all accompanied by their wives except for Billy, who was divorced—headed out to the famed

New York nightspot to celebrate Billy's 29th birthday. Sammy Davis Jr. was the headliner that evening, and a group of guys from a bowling league, also out to celebrate, began heckling Davis, allegedly using racial slurs. The Yankees stood up for Sammy, words were exchanged, then fists. When the dust cleared, one of the hecklers was left with both a concussion and a broken jaw. (Evidence indicates Hank Bauer, a decorated ex-Marine, was responsible.) Although the subsequent lawsuit against the Yankee players never made it out of a grand jury hearing, the incident was a black eye for the club, and George Weiss and other management personnel laid much of the blame on Martin.

I wasn't there. That night, Moose Skowron and I had volunteered to babysit for Hank Bauer and his wife so they could go. Moose was a pure athlete and a straight-arrow, always in bed by 10 or 11 p.m, so he was the perfect guy for the job.

I can't tell you if Billy Martin was the main instigator that night. What I *can* tell you is that he had a short fuse, and that he and Sammy Davis Jr. were good friends. A lover of the nightlife, Billy was chummy with a lot of the top-drawer entertainers, including Sammy, as I found out one long night in early August. Kansas City was finishing up a three-game series against the White Sox in Chicago. It was a Thursday getaway day, and we were supposed to get on a midnight train to Cleveland following the afternoon game.

Sammy Davis Jr. happened to be performing at a club in Chicago that night, and Billy said, "Hey, Ralph. Let's go see Sammy."

"Great," I said. So we caught the first show, met with Sammy afterwards, and we were talking and having a good time when Sammy said, "Why don't you guys stay for the second show? You really ought to stay for the second show."

I knew if we stayed, we'd miss the train. But that didn't concern Billy.

"Aw, don't worry about it," he told me. "We'll go over in the morning."

So we stayed. That morning of August 9, we were up at 7:30 to get on a plane run by Capitol Airlines for a one-hour hop over to Cleveland. We ended up walking into the hotel at the same time the rest of the team was getting off the train. Nobody even missed us.

I happened to be pitching that night, matched up against Cleveland ace Early Wynn. With two outs in the ninth inning, I was leading 2-1. Then Roger Maris, a Cleveland Indian at the time, stepped up and launched one off the top of the fence in right field for a score-tying home run. We went into extra innings, and I stayed in the game until the end of the 11th. I was pulled for a pinch-hitter—Irv Noren, the guy whose injury had paved the way for my Yankee debut the season before. Now he, like me, was a Kansas City Athletic. He'd come over with Mickey McDermott in that trade I mentioned earlier.

We didn't score, and Virgil Trucks came in to relieve me. Then, in the 13th, we finally got a run and won, 3-2.

I guess it's only right that the run was driven in by none other than my nightclubbing partner of the night before, Billy Martin.

06

THE MASTER

Earlier, I wrote about meeting Ted Williams during spring training in '54, my first year of pro ball, when the Yankees and Red Sox shared the same facilities at Sarasota, Florida. I saw him the next year, too, in the same locker room, and he asked me what kind of season I'd had.

"I won eight out of my last 10," I told him. "I think they're going to send me to Denver."

"That's good," he said. "Sounds like you're doing all right."

Williams was in the last few years of his career then, still one of the greatest players to ever take the field. A story from a long time ago may be apocryphal, but it gives an idea of what a threat Williams was at the plate. As I heard it, Williams had come up and hit a home run his first at-bat. The next time, he hit a triple, The third time, a double. Then, his fourth time up, he's got a three and two count and the pitcher throws a borderline pitch.

"Ball four!" shouts the umpire.

The pitcher heads toward the plate, raising hell, and the umpire calmly says, "I don't know what you're complaining about. At least *I* held him to one base."

A legendary guy like that didn't have to give a young minor leaguer the time of day. But he actually seemed interested in me, and I got to know him a little bit. Later, when I'd made it to the majors and we'd play Boston, I'd go around behind the batting cage during practice and talk to him.

I remember the advice he gave me one time when I asked him what to do about those pesky little leadoff hitters I was facing, guys like Harvey Kuenn in Detroit and Nellie Fox for the White Sox.

"Bunch your defense," he told me. "Bring your right fielder and your left fielder in and bunch the defense up the middle. Then, just smoke it over the plate and let 'em tee off. Show them a little slider or curve every once in awhile, just to keep them thinking, but don't try to outsmart 'em. They're smarter than you are. Those little sons of bitches don't strike out ten times a year."

Williams cussed quite a bit. And when he did, it had an almost beautiful quality to it.

Another time, I met him behind the batting cage, and he said, "So how's it going, kid?"

I said, "You know, every time I start, I'm having trouble the first couple of innings. I'll put a couple of guys on, and then I'll give up a three-run homer. I'm not getting out of the early innings."

I wasn't really asking for advice; I was just telling him what was going on. But he gave me some good counsel anyway.

"Look," he told me, "you get a couple of men on in an early inning and then groove one to a power hitter, he's *going* to hit a three-run homer. Then, like you say, you've dug a big hole for yourself and your club. If you've got a power hitter up there and you're missing your spots, not getting the ball where you want to, start working the outside corner. If you miss, miss outside. Make him hit it over the centerfield fence. There aren't six guys in this league who can hit it over the centerfield fence. Mantle. Skowron."

"Williams?" I asked.

"Williams," he said, and then named three more.

"You realize," he added, "you can walk four guys in a row to get to that out man who couldn't hit you if you threw a basketball up there. You're going to have the number of at least one guy in the lineup, and if you have to walk four guys to get to him, that's only one run, and you're out of a jam."

That advice may have been unorthodox, but it struck me as really good thinking.

Ted Williams and Casey Stengel were the only two guys I knew who thought outside the box like that. Casey was into statistics. He had a guy working for him who could tell him how many times a particular player had struck out, or hit into a double play, that kind of stuff. Casey would play percentages. He'd go into Fenway Park with a starting lineup of all left-handed hitters, because the Red Sox had a lot of right-handed pitchers, all of whom were in the habit of throwing outside to right-handed hitters, to keep them from pulling the ball to the Green Monster in left field. On the other hand, the bullpen in right field line was a close shot. The Boston pitchers were so geared to pitching right-handed batters outside that they'd make a lot of pitches to that side of the plate, sometimes by accident, which meant they'd come inside on lefties, giving them a better shot at the bullpen in right. It really screwed them up to pitch to left-handers.

Then again, Fenway was just a tough place to pitch. I remember getting knocked out there one time in the early innings. I came into the clubhouse all pissed off, and Lefty Gomez was there. One of the great Yankee pitchers of the '30s and early '40s, he was then traveling for Wilson Sporting Goods, going to all the major league clubs and getting the measurements of players for their uniforms.

"How you doin', kid?" he asked me.

"This Fenway Park's too small for me," I said. "I like the confines of Yankee Stadium."

"Ralph, do you know the secret to pitching in Fenway?"

"No," I told him. "What is it?"

"You've got to spend half an hour in a closet before you go out to pitch, so the park'll look big to you. And you need to watch out when you come sidearm or you'll scrape your knuckles on the Green Monster."

Casey reversed himself when he went into Brooklyn for the World Series. At one point, he started almost all right-handed hitters. Ebbetts Field had a short right porch. Because it was only about 300 feet to the right-field pole, the Dodgers pitchers had gotten used to pitching away from left-handed hitters and inside to right-handers. In '56, the last of the four times Brooklyn and the Yankees met while Casey was the manager, Yogi was the only left-handed batter in the starting lineup. He was the one who won the game, though, hitting three home runs with eight RBIs in the four times he faced the Dodgers' top pitcher, Don Newcombe.

All those Dodgers pitchers were throwing low and outside, which was the way to keep left-handed batters from muscling it over the right field fence. But when Casey stacked the lineup with right-handed hitters, those same pitchers were throwing right into the batters' power zones.

Casey also had a thing about putting fireballers like Ryne Duren, who threw a hundred miles an hour, into a game. "I don't ever want to bring 'em in with the bases loaded," he told me once. "I always like to have a base open, so they'll have a chance to get their feet on the ground and find the strike zone. Once they're in the zone, they'll either get a swing and a miss or a popup, and when the smoke clears, the tying run'll still be on third base."

Casey Stengel really was an innovator. He was a pioneer of the platoon system, which a lot of guys didn't like because it robbed them of playing time and sometimes kept their batting averages down. It also helped control salaries, although I don't think Casey did it for that reason. He did it because it worked. He'd say, "Come September, you show me a manager who doesn't platoon his players, and I'll show you a manager who's in the second division." He never platooned up the middle, with his center fielder, shortstop, second-baseman, and catcher, but he did it at all the other positions.

Casey made the transition from the dead-ball era, where you bunted, hit and run, stole bases, and brought old veterans in to relieve starters. His relievers were low-ball pitchers who could throw curves—they didn't necessarily have to throw hard, but they needed to be able to come in and get a batter to hit a ground ball.

As for Ted Williams—I didn't just get advice from him. I also had to pitch to him for four years, from 1956 through '60, when he retired after batting .316 his final season. The first year I faced him, he was seven for 10 against me. Then I started doing some research. There was an ex-major league relief pitcher named Marlin Stuart who'd been a teammate of mine on the Denver Bears in '55. He had a good sinkerball, which was pretty much all he pitched; he'd throw it outside and it would really tail away down around the knees. He'd had pretty good luck with Williams.

Then there was another ex-major leaguer, Earl Caldwell, who lived down in the Rio Grande Valley in Texas, which happened to be where my dad and brother were living at the time. I visited Earl, and he told me he'd had some luck throwing Williams a screwball.

The A's had a pitching coach named Spud Chandler who'd been a dominant Yankee right-hander during the early years of World War II. Even though the pitch was normally associated with southpaws, because not a lot of righties could make the ball move that way, he had thrown a screwball with a lot of success. He'd also done it right. A lot of pitchers would snap it, really cranking their arms, which put stress and strain on their elbows and often led to injuries. But Spud showed me the way he did it, with a special little grip on the ball that he twisted in his hand and then flipped, using a lot of wrist.

Believe it or not, I got Ted Williams out with that pitch. The very first time I threw it to him, he hit a popup to short. He just didn't expect it, coming from me, and he really didn't know what the hell it was. The next time, I threw him another screwball, and he hit another little pop fly, this time to short right field. The third time, he'd adjusted. I had two strikes on him, and he was ready and waiting for the new pitch—so I threw him a fastball and struck him out. It was the first time I'd ever fanned Ted Williams.

After the game, I asked him, "How'd you like that pitch?"

"Well, it's not overpowering," he said, "so don't use it all the time. But it'll be really good for you if you slip it in there every once in a while. Just don't get away from your basic pitches, the ones that have given you your success."

Years afterward, near the end of my baseball career, I'd end up teaching the screwball to someone who'd save his career with it. That, though, is a story for a later chapter.

* * * *

I finished up the 1957 season 5-12: 1-1 with the Yankees and 4-11 with the Kansas City A's, who ended up 59-94. That was good for seventh place in the American League, 4 and a half games ahead of cellar-dwelling Washington. My won-lost record was hardly stellar, but I had a good ERA of 3.33 to go with it. Returning to Chelsea after the season's end, I planned to take some more college courses in the off-season before spring training.

One very early Sunday morning, those plans changed.

It was November 10, 1957. I was driving back from Tulsa, a distance of about 50 miles, on old Route 66, and I was really drowsy. I remember seeing the lights of Claremore, a town about 18 miles from home, in the distance. I guess I nodded off after that for a few seconds, because when I looked at the speedometer I saw I was doing 95 miles an hour and gaining hard on the car in front of me. Slamming on the brakes, I swerved just in time to miss it, but I couldn't straighten myself out. I shot off the highway and went airborne into a valley, one of the few along that stretch. The car and I rolled through the air four or five times, and in the few seconds before it hit, I had the presence of mind to flatten out and double up in the seat, knowing if I kept sitting up, my head would probably be smashed.

I woke up to the sound of the wheels still spinning, *whoom, whoom*. My car was on its side, the radio still playing, the smashed-up radiator hissing steam. I lay beside it, thrown into a wet and muddy patch of ground. Slowly, I moved my hands over my body, trying to feel if all the parts were still there. It took a while.

Once I was convinced I was all together, I tried to stand up. I guess I'd hit and skidded through the mud once I was ejected from the car, because my pants were down around my ankles. Then I began to realize that I couldn't get my legs to move. I was paralyzed from the waist down.

"Uh-oh," I remember thinking. "I've got a broken back." Then I started shivering. I didn't know it at the time, but I was in shock. That and the cold temperature, along with my sense of panic, had caused a temporary paralysis. My body had just shut down.

So I lay there in the mud, shaking, until a trucker spotted me from the highway, pulled over, and ran down to where I was. He had a tarp in his rig, and he put it over me and then called Claremore on his two-way radio. Before long, a rescue squad came rolling in. I'll never forget one of them looking me in the eyes—he was a baseball player I knew. He said, "Oh, my God. It's *Ralph*."

As they loaded me up to take me to the hospital, I remember thinking, "Well, I wonder what I'll be doing for a living *now*?" I was pretty sure it wasn't going to be baseball any more.

Once they got me to the hospital, they laid me out on a cold slab to take some X-rays. There was a kid there from Oklahoma Military

Academy, a school just outside of Claremore, who'd OD'd on something, taken too many pills, and they'd just pumped his stomach out, so it was a little while before they could get to me. I didn't have much choice but to lie there and shiver.

Finally, they began working on me, and when they were finished with the X-rays, they put me in bed, in traction. My doctor—I believe his name was Daugherty—said, "Our radiologist doesn't come in until Monday. That's when he'll read your X-rays." So I spent the night in that hospital bed, wondering about a lot of things, including my future.

That next morning a young doctor came in and looked over the X-rays. He left and came back with Dr. Daugherty, who told me that he had good news.

"You don't have a broken hip," he said. "You can get up and walk."

Well, that *was* good news. Until I hoisted myself up and tried to take a step—and suddenly felt knives stabbing me. It was the most excruciating pain I'd ever felt.

"Something's wrong," the doctor said quickly. "Get back in bed."

I lay there, waiting for the pain to subside. Something *was* wrong, no doubt about it.

There was a clinic at St. Luke's Hospital in Kansas City, the Dixon-Diveley Clinic, that took care of the A's players. It was the No. 1 orthopedic health center in the Midwest. So they put me in an ambulance in Claremore and drove me all the way up to Kansas City, a distance of about 250 miles. I remember the ride alone cost $75. Once I was there, they X-rayed me at all kinds of different angles and found out that I had a fracture around the rim of my left hip socket. Apparently, when I was thrown from my car, my knee had hit the ground and jammed back into my hip socket—my left *acetabulum*, to be technical—cracking the rim. The crack went into the socket about half an inch and then alongside it for about an inch and a half.

Things didn't look very good. They started telling me about how they could put in various devices, balls and things, to allow me to walk again. They kept me in traction for over two months, on my back, the weight on my stretched-out left leg. They'd take new X-rays every week or so, paying special attention to the head of the femur. If it turned gray, that meant the bone had ossified, and once it did, they had to go in and clip it off. It sounded to me like a medieval operation.

Then one day, Dr. Paul Meyer—a founding partner in the clinic—came by to see me. And this time the news really *was* good.

"We're not going to have to rebuild that hip after all," he told me. "You never lost circulation in your femur, so you won't lose the hip. You're going to play ball again."

Before it was all over, I'd spent eleven weeks in traction. As I went along, they changed the setup to a wheel with a weight on it, attached to my boot. And finally, I was able to get up and start walking.

Just about the time I was recovered enough to start getting around pretty well, Dodgers catcher Roy Campanella had his one-car accident, skidding on a patch of ice while driving back to his Long Island home from his off-season job managing a liquor store in Harlem. It happened on January 28, 1958, breaking his neck and ending his playing days. He had to use a wheelchair for the rest of his life.

So as bad as my wreck had been, I knew it could've been a whole lot worse, and I felt awful for Roy Campanella, already a star, with who knows how many more years of baseball snatched away from him in seconds on that icy New York road.

* * * *

I went to camp with the Athletics a little early that year. Their regular spring training was in Palm Beach, but they had an early camp in Haines

FRONT ROW: Whitey Herzog, Bob Davis, Ray Herbert, Coach Bob Swift, Mgr. Harry Craft, Coach Spurgeon Chandler, Don Heffner, Jack Urban, Mike Baxes, Murry Dickson, Batboy Dale Close (seated); MIDDLE ROW: Trainer Jim Ewell, Bob Grim, Hal Smith, Chico Carrasquel, Harry Simpson, Preston Ward, Ralph Terry, Harry Chiti, Bud Daley, Dave Keefe, Clay Reid; BACK ROW: Ned Garver, Hector Lopez, Walt Craddock, Roger Maris, Dick Tomanek, Bill Tuttle, Joe DeMaestri, Bob Martyn, Bob Cerv, Tom Gorman, Frank House.

City, Florida, and that's the one I checked into. My hip was still not 100 percent weight-bearing, so I couldn't do any running. I'd play a little pepper, a little soft-toss, and that was about it.

A couple of the Kansas City coaches, the old Detroit catcher Bob Swift and former Browns infielder Don Hefner, were avid golfers. That was a game I'd never picked up, although I'd go out and watch them play. At one point, one of them said, "Look, Ralph, why don't you just rent a set of clubs, carry 'em around with you, and play some golf? That'd help get your legs in shape."

It sounded like a good idea to me. So every day at noon they'd let me out of practice, and I'd go over to the Haines City Municipal Course, which was full of big trees draped with Spanish moss, and rent some old clubs and a bag, get some balls, and go out to the course. At first, like a lot of people, I hit nothing but grounders. I hit grounders until I was sick of them, and then I started getting balls airborne. The guys at the course showed me how to correct my slice and get out of sand traps, and I was on my way. I'd play until dark every night. It was good therapy, and it helped me get back in shape.

Little did I know that it would also be a big part of my life *after* baseball.

* * * *

Thanks in great part to my daily golf games, I got in shape and was ready to pitch when the 1958 season rolled around. Although we'd end the year in seventh place, just ahead of the Senators again, we were a better team, winning 14 more games than we had the year before. Bud Daley, Ray Herbert, veteran Ned Garver—who'd won 20 games in '51 pitching for a last-place team, the old St. Louis Browns—and I made up the nucleus of a good pitching staff. Our shortstop-second base combo was solid, with Joe DeMaestri and Hector Lopez, respectively, and we even had a little power, mostly from Bob Cerv, who hit 38 home runs and knocked in 104 RBIs that year. Midway through the season, we picked up another slugger from Cleveland, trading away our starting first baseman, Vic Power, and outfielder Woodie Held for him, first baseman-outfielder Preston Ward, who replaced Power at first, and pitcher Dick Tomanek. The guy's name was Roger Maris, and he made an immediate impact on our ballclub.

I won 11 games for the A's that year, losing 13. I was 10-11, going pretty good, when I lost both ends of a doubleheader to the Yankees in mid-September, playing in Kansas City. I started the first game and was trailing 4-0 after five innings when our manager, Harry Craft, gave me the hook. We lost 5-3. The second game went extra innings. Harry sent me out there in the 10th inning, and I pitched four and two-thirds of an inning more. The Yankees won that one 12-7, and I was charged with the loss.

My dad had come up from Texas to see me play, which was a first for him. He'd seen me play twice in the minors, once at Little Rock, when I was with Birmingham in the Southern League, and then in Wichita, when I was pitching for the Denver Bears. But never in the major leagues.

Although dad had played a little ball himself—or maybe *because* of it—he was of the old mindset that baseball wasn't a true profession. He figured if you played ball, you were shirking when you should be working. I'd thought about that early on, but when I saw that baseball had a pension plan, I thought, "We're entering a modern, high-speed society, where there's going to be a shorter work week, and recreation is going to play a very important part in people's lives. They're going to need diversions and entertainment, and baseball will help supply that." Of course, I was going to play ball anyway, so maybe I was just justifying it to myself.

The day Dad saw me, the teams spent about eight hours on the field, and he sat through every pitch. Afterwards, he said, "Well, I guess you *do* work for a living."

It was the last time he ever saw me pitch.

Ralph Terry at the National Baseball
Players' Championship Golf Tournament.
February 1962, Miami, Florida.

07

MY ZEN

While going to NEO in Miami, Oklahoma, during the off-season, I'd met a young woman from Seneca, Missouri, named Julia Boehning. After NEO, we'd both gone to Southwest Missouri State at Springfield. She'd become like a sister to me. And like any sister, she had ideas about what was best for her "brother."

In 1958, Julia was working as an airline hostess for TWA, and one day she told me she had found just the right person for me to date. It didn't matter at all to her that I was seeing someone else at the time.

"You're not going with the right gal," Julia explained. "I'm working with someone who's just perfect for you."

That someone turned out to be Tanya Simmons, another hostess, and Julia just raved about her. She kept it up for about two months until I finally said okay, I'll ask her out. I didn't know until later that Julia had been working on Tanya as hard as she'd been working on me. She really wanted us to get together.

So finally, when the A's were playing on our home field at Municipal Stadium in Kansas City, I called Tanya and told her I'd leave her a couple tickets at the window so she could go to one of our games and bring a friend,

YOUNG LOVE
Tanya and Ralph

then we'd meet face to face after it was over. I left two because I figured if she didn't like the way I looked or something, she wouldn't be stuck and she'd have someone she could leave with.

"Meet me down by the rightfield corner after the game," I said, "about 15 or 20 minutes after the crowd clears out."

After we'd played, I cleaned up, changed clothes, and went out to look for her in the place I'd mentioned. No one was there. On the way, I'd passed a girl who was standing in the crowd with another girl, and I'd thought, "Boy, I wish *that* was her."

Finally, just about everyone had cleared out of the stadium. And lo and behold, here were those two young women I'd seen. I went up to the one who'd caught my eye earlier and said, "Are you Tanya?"

"Yes. Are you Ralph?"

She was with an old friend from her hometown of Larned, Kansas, Pat Douglas, who said hello and then discreetly faded away. I took Tanya to a late-hours place, Jimmy & Mary's in downtown Kansas City, for a bite to eat. It became clear pretty quickly that we had a lot in common, including our small-town roots.

I remember when I first knew she was the one for me. It was the off-season, and I was once again continuing my education by taking classes, this time at the University of Kansas City. One evening we went to a little place called Sidney's and walked around the Plaza in Kansas City, talking about her job, and about baseball and where I was going. We talked all night. From the beginning, there'd never been any question about her looks, and I was very attracted to her, but that was the first time that we'd really gotten to know one another.

Even though we knew we were compatible and comfortable in each other's company, we didn't rush things. It would be a couple more years before we got engaged, and another several months before we took the plunge and got married.

It was not only plenty of time for us to find out whether we were really compatible or not. It was also enough time for my professional life to take another turn or two.

* * * *

Although the 1959 A's started the season with the same starting rotation of Daley, Garver, Herbert, and me, and had both Cerv and Maris providing power—with new third baseman Dick Williams, who'd come over from the Orioles in a straight-up trade for infielder Chico Carrasquel, showing some pop, too—they won seven fewer games than they had the year before. The team finished 66-88 in '59, once again in seventh place, sandwiched between the Orioles in sixth and the traditionally dead-last Washington Senators.

By that time, though, I wasn't in KC any more. Neither was the team's first-string second baseman, Hector Lopez. In May of '59, we'd been traded to the Yankees for pitchers Johnny Kucks and Tom Sturdivant and infielder Jerry Lumpe.

I remember when Hector and I got the word. It was a rainy night in Kansas City, just before the second of a two-game series with the Detroit Tigers. Neither team had taken batting practice, and the gates hadn't yet been opened to let the crowds in. Hector and I were in the dugout when Harry Craft, our manager, came over and said he needed to talk to Hector and me. We went underneath the grandstand over behind first base, out of the rain, and he told us that the team had just made a trade.

There had been rumors that the two of us were going to Boston or Cleveland, so the trade wasn't unexpected—only our destination.

"Where are we going?" I asked him.

"Well, you're going to New York for Lumpe, Sturdivant, and Kucks."

Hector and I looked at each other. He had to be excited about becoming a Yankee, and I was happy about putting the pinstripes on again. Once they'd gotten rid of someone, the Yankees very seldom traded back for him.

Harry gave us that news on the evening of May 26, a Tuesday. Right away, we headed for New York, where Casey was waiting to greet us.

"I got rid of you, kid," he told me. "Now I've got you back. And you're pitching Thursday night against Baltimore."

I started that game against their knuckleballing ace Hoyt Wilhelm and pitched seven innings, giving up three earned runs. We lost 5-0, which meant that I had a 2-5 record for the year so far, but over the season Casey gave me more chances to improve those stats, starting me in 15 more games and using me as a reliever in eight. Once I went over to New York, Don Larsen and I battled all year for that fifth starter's job, behind Whitey Ford, Art Ditmar, Bob Turley, and Duke Maas.

Meanwhile, Hector became the Yankees' starting third baseman, moving over from second to accommodate the rising star Bobby Richardson. Although he'd been named to the All-Star Team in '57, 1959 was the year Bobby really broke out, playing in 134 games and getting more than 500 plate appearances for the first time in his major league career.

Bobby Richardson was one of what I like to call the quiet leaders on the Yankees. When I'd get in a little jam, he'd be the first one out to the mound, and he'd say, "Just make 'em hit it on the ground, Ralph, and we'll get you a double play." He never raised his voice, never cussed at you.

Clete Boyer was another quiet leader, and so was Elston Howard. It's hard to believe Elston was the very first black player on the Yankees, but he was, and he spent his first few years in New York as kind of a super utility man. While he'd end up being the main Yankee catcher during the 1960 season, when I rejoined the team in '59, Yogi was getting most of the starts behind the plate. But Casey always found a way to get Elston into games. He'd platoon him with Moose Skowron at first base, or he'd put him in left field. Even though Elston played all those different positions in '59, he was still named to the second of the two American League All-Star Teams that played against the National League that year, as were Richardson and Berra. (It's a testament to the strength and depth of the Yankees that both Skowron and Howard, listed as first basemen, made that All-Star roster, as did Richardson and Gil McDougald, both primarily second basemen, although McDougald played at other spots around the infield. It's not often that two teammates who played the same position, other than pitchers, went to the All-Star Game together.)

Like Bobby, Elston didn't raise his voice. He'd come out to the mound and say, "Just get 'em out and we'll win this game for you." When you were in a jam, he'd always try to get you to push a little harder, give a little extra effort. Elston always rooted for you to get through it.

Yogi was a little different. If he thought you were getting tired, especially if the team was losing, he had a signal worked out with Casey. He'd look over to the dugout and communicate without words that he needed a fresh horse out there.

Of course, all of us pitchers knew it. In 1959, as I worked to stay in the starting rotation, I felt like Casey—we called him the Old Man—was taking me out too early and not trusting me to work out of jams on my own. One day I was talking to Yogi about it, and he asked, "So you'd like to stay in these games a little longer?"

"Sure," I told him.

"Okay. When the Old Man comes out to the mound, don't start a conversation with him. Don't say *anything.*"

Like most pitchers, I never wanted to come out of a game. So when Stengel got to the mound and gave me a quizzical look, I'd always say something like, "I feel good. I think I can get this guy." More often than not, though, he'd turn to the bullpen and signal for a fresh arm, pretty much ignoring what I'd said.

To an extent, I understood. It could be embarrassing for a manager to leave his pitcher in. Sometimes the next guy up would get an RBI, maybe even hit one out of the park, and then the manager would have to make that long trudge back to the mound and do what he'd wanted to do a batter earlier.

So Yogi told me, "Remember. Let him open the conversation."

The next start after we had that talk, I was in a little trouble and here came Casey. I stood there, not saying anything, stalling, and Casey didn't say anything either. We stood there, silently, until the plate umpire came out and said, "What's it going to be, Case?"

Finally, he turned to me. "How do you feel?" he asked.

"Okay," I told him.

"Well, then, *curve* this sunde bitch." That's how he always said it: *sunde* bitch. And he walked back to the dugout.

By that time, I did have a better curveball, which Yankee pitching coach Jim Turner had helped me develop. In between my two New York stints with Turner, who was very good on the fundamentals, I'd also learned from Spud Chandler and then Johnny Sain, his successor, at Kansas City.

NEW YORK YANKEES
1960 AMERICAN LEAGUE CHAMPIONS

First Row, Left to Right: GIL McDOUGALD, BILL SKOWRON, BOBBY RICHARDSON, JIM HEGAN, EDDIE LOPAT, FRANK CROSETTI, CASEY STENGEL, RALPH HOUK, JOHNNY BLANCHARD, ELSTON HOWARD, YOGI BERRA.
Second Row, Left to Right: JOE SOARES, CLETIS BOYER, JOE DEMAESTRI, TONY KUBEK, DALE LONG, HECTOR LOPEZ, BOB CERV, MICKEY MANTLE, ROGER MARIS, GUS MAUCH.
Third Row, Left to Right: LUIS ARROYO, DUKE MAAS, ELI GRBA, RYNE DUREN, BILL STAFFORD, JIM COATES, RALPH TERRY, BOB TURLEY, ART DITMAR, WHITEY FORD, BOBBY SHANTZ.
Seated on Ground in Front: Batboys FRANK PRUDENTI, FRED BENGIS.

After his great years as a pitcher with the Braves in the late '40s and early '50s, Sain had racked up some pretty good years with the Yankees before turning to coaching. I'd actually been in spring training with him when I first started my pro career, in '54 and again in '55.

One of the greatest all-time pitchers, Bob Feller, also gave me a couple of tips. He was never an official coach, but after his playing days ended in '56, he just seemed to be around, showing up at old-timers' games and events like that.

As stellar as his career was, it would've been even more impressive if he hadn't lost almost four seasons to military service during World War II. I've read that he was the first professional athlete to enlist after Pearl Harbor, and he saw combat while he was aboard the battleship USS Alabama. It's now docked at Battleship Memorial Park in Mobile,

Alabama, where visitors can go aboard and explore the vessel that had Feller on its crew. I went there once and found his bunk, which has a little plaque affixed to it noting that Bob Feller slept there.

All the time he was in the Navy, Feller worked out on the deck, with a guy catching him, so he could stay in shape. It worked, and he was able to resume his career with the Cleveland Indians for many more years. Before he volunteered for the service, however, he was the pitcher in an American League contest that makes for a great trivia question: When was the only game ever played in the big leagues in which none of the batting averages on one of the teams went up or down?

The answer: Bob Feller's no-hitter on Opening Day, 1940, when he blanked the White Sox 1-0. It remains the only Opening Day no-hitter ever.

I still remember a conversation I had with Feller many decades ago, when I asked him how I could keep left-handers from pulling the ball.

"Start your curveball off the plate and break it in," he told me. "Just catch the outside corner—a back-door curve. Then, follow that up with a curve you throw a little bit harder—a slider, or a slurve—and throw it a little bit farther outside. To the batter, it *looks* like it's going to come over the plate, but it stays out there. It's also a little bit faster, so if the batter commits, he's going to be late, and instead of pulling it to right, he'll hit it to centerfield, and there won't be much on it because he's had to reach and he's gotten to it late."

As I went along, I learned lots of little nuances, little tricks like that, keeping my ears open and paying attention. Another thing I picked up was the psychology of pitching inside. You didn't necessarily throw inside to scare or intimidate a batter. You did it to *bait* him. He'd think, "Uh-oh, he's coming inside on me. I'll be ready." That set him up for an outside pitch.

Then the guy would switch gears. "Oops, he got me with one on the outside. If he does that again, I'll be waiting for him."

You had to tease 'em. And it was all predicated on control. If you didn't have control of your pitches, all of the theory in the world wouldn't help you at all. On the other hand, even the very top pitchers are not always going to get the ball to go where they want it to go, I don't care *how* good they are. In fact, the most infamous single pitch I ever threw is one of those that just didn't go where I'd planned, as you'll see in the next chapter.

* * * *

In his very accurate 2008 book, *The Yankees in the Early 1960s,* author William J. Ryczek writes about how I always used to carry a baseball around with me, which is true. I used it as a symbol, to sharpen my concentration and get me in game mode. It started when Jim Turner changed my grip on the curveball, moving it up a little bit so I'd get more spin. I really had to concentrate to get it right, and it took some time.

I've never really talked about this before, because I'm sure some people will think it's bullshit, but the idea to keep a ball in my hand for long periods of time came from a college psychology class. Although I never got a degree, I went to college for seven years, usually doing one semester every off-season, occasionally getting in a couple before the start of the next baseball season. I was particularly interested in social studies, history, and psychology, and it was in a psychology class that I first studied the writings of Adler and Jung. I was fascinated by the potential power these two great thinkers said was in us all. We've all heard those stories about a man or woman lifting a burning car off someone trapped underneath it. Adler figured that power was summoned from a conscious level, but Jung said it was more ritualistic — that the fire was an archetypal symbol that triggered a sudden superhuman ability.

When the Yankees changed my grip on the curveball, I got the idea to develop my *own* symbol. I had come up with kind of a lazy curve in high school, and it was pretty simple to throw because the balls were roughed up and easy to handle. In the majors, though, they were smooth and new, so I couldn't curve them as well. When Jim Turner moved my grip up and

Ralph in the dugout during the Yankees' 1960 season.

I started working on what he wanted me to do, holding the ball and turning it over in my hand, I got the idea to use the baseball itself as a symbol. So before every game, I'd sit at my locker, spinning the ball, counting the 106 stitches, and think about what was coming up, just to narrow my focus and get my mind off all the distractions.

I wasn't the only person on the Yankees who tried unorthodox ways to try and get an edge. Our skinny little infielder Phil Linz is best known for the so-called "harmonica incident" with Yogi on the team bus in 1964, which we'll go into later in the book. But he also went through a period when he was working on self-hypnosis. He'd go into the head, shut the door, and concentrate, telling himself, "You'll get a good pitch to hit. You'll be patient." Stuff like that. He'd tell himself all the good things he was going to do, and he actually got to the point of being able to put himself in a little bit of a trance.

So one day we were playing in Washington after the old Senators had moved to Minnesota and the league had formed a new Senators team via expansion. Clete Boyer had a headache or some other ailment, so he was scratched and Linz started at third base. When he found out, he headed to the washroom, put himself into a trance, and came out ready to play.

Linz was a line-drive hitter, a singles hitter. But that day he hit a ball into the upper deck of the stadium, where nobody but people like Mantle and Frank Howard could drive it. He played great in the field and went three for four at the plate. He was on fire.

The problem was, the next day or two he couldn't do much of anything. He was all uncoordinated and weak. The self-hypnosis had helped him achieve his maximum potential, but it had also taken too much out of him.

I remember hearing a story about the old St. Louis Browns, who were a last-place team pretty much every year. One time management brought in a hypnotist to help their players. The hypnotist would say things like,

"You're better than DiMaggio," pumping them up, telling them what great players they were.

But it didn't work. They just weren't that good.

* * * *

I ended up starting 19 games for the Yankees in '59, going 3-7. Again, not a great win-loss record, but a good ERA of 3.39 and a complete-game shutout to go with it. Putting my A's and Yankees stats together, I had 1959 season totals of 5-11, with a 3.89 ERA.

I also made a little bit of history during that season, although I didn't know it at the time. It happened during a game at Yankee Stadium against the White Sox on July 17, and it was a dandy. Neither Chicago ace Early Wynn—who'd go on to win the Cy Young Award that year—nor I allowed a hit until the bottom of the sixth, when I led off and grounded a ball to deep short. Luis Aparicio fielded it and threw to first base, but I barely beat the throw and was called safe.

Mel Allen was the Yankees' television announcer then, and since it was not only a close play but the first hit of the entire ballgame, he said, "I wonder if they could show that again?" So he asked his cameraman, and he backed up the videotape and re-showed my hit. That's gone down in history as the first instant replay ever on TV.

I've seen some references that say the instant replay was used after the White Sox's right fielder, Jim McAnany, got the Sox's first hit against me. I had a no-hitter through eight innings, but McAnany led off and hit a ground ball that went right through my legs and out to center field. There was no doubt that it was a hit, so there was no need for a replay.

I gave up another hit that inning, to centerfielder Jim Landis, and finished with a complete-game two-hitter. So did Wynn. But the Sox won, 2-0, to give me my final loss of the season.

Casey Stengel instructs his
young pitcher Ralph Terry

Nineteen-fifty-nine was a disappointing year for the Yankees. After winning it all in the World Series against the Milwaukee Braves in '58, we dropped to third place in the American League, 15 games out of first and 10 games behind the second place Cleveland Indians. Instead of us, it was the Chicago White Sox going to the fall classic for the first time in 40 years, squaring off against the Los Angeles Dodgers.

The day after the season ended, I went back to the clubhouse to clean out my locker and get a dozen baseballs, my glove, and one of Yogi's old catcher's mitts, things I needed to be able to work out in the off-season.

At that time, the NFL's New York Giants, then coached by the old Arkansawyer Jim Lee Howell, played their home games at Yankee Stadium. The team always scheduled its first five games of the season on the road, because we were usually in the World Series and our management didn't want football players out there tearing up the sod. So the Giants started every season training up in the Bronx, at Fordham. But the minute the Yankees' season was over, they moved right into our lockers.

When I came into the clubhouse, they were already there. As I was stacking up my stuff, Sam Huff, the middle linebacker, and Dick Modzelewski, a big tackle, came over and grabbed up the gloves and one of the balls and started playing catch, right there in the locker room. It wasn't long before they were throwing harder and harder, playing burnout, with the other guys in there cheering them on. The locker room had pretty dim lighting, and an accident could've easily happened. I don't care how big and tough you are—if a baseball hits you in the teeth, it can do some damage.

So there they were, firing at each other as hard as they could, making a lot of noise, and I wasn't at all sure how it was going to end. Then Howell's two assistant coaches, Tom Landry and Vince Lombardi, came around the corner and saw what was going on.

"All right," Lombardi bellowed immediately. "Knock that shit *off!*"

And boy, they did. They handed me the gloves and the ball and sat right down.

After the close of the season, I went into the Army to fulfill my military obligation. In 1955, President Eisenhower had signed into law something called the Reserve Forces Act, which was intended to build up a trained military reserve at home that could be mobilized in case of a national emergency. If you were drafted, you had to serve two years in the military. But if you joined the Army's RFA program, as it was called, you only had to do six months as a full-time soldier. Even though it came with an eight-year obligation in the Army Reserve, only three of those years were active, meaning that you had to attend 48 drill meetings and a two-week summer training camp in each of them. So it was a good deal for guys who didn't want their lives and work completely disrupted for a full two years. In addition, those with seasonal jobs—like baseball players—

could apply for early release from active duty. If you could show that failure to show up for baseball spring training or frog-hunting season or whatever else might seriously handicap your future earning power, you had a great shot at getting out early.

So I enlisted and was ordered to report to Fort Leonard Wood in Missouri. I stayed there for about four and a half months, saving up all my leave time, and then applied for early release so I could go to spring training.

Even though I was certainly not asking for any special treatment and was clearly entitled to early release—other ballplayers all around me were getting out under the exact same circumstances—the Army for some reason denied my application.

Tanya, who visited me several times at the Army base, had an uncle named Tony Schartz, a four-time state representative in her home state of Kansas. He was a very popular guy, a Democrat in Republican country, who usually ran unopposed. He sold Case farm implements and storage bins, things like that, and he knew everybody. The farmers loved him, but he and his brother didn't get along too well. In fact, Tony only had one eye, thanks to a pitchfork fight the two of them had gotten into when they were both kids.

We did some pheasant hunting together, Tony and I. He had a little 28 gauge shotgun, smaller than a .410, and for a guy with one eye, he could shoot very well. We'd talk a lot about baseball. He loved the sport. He even had a little bitty curveball that he'd throw to me when we played catch.

Tony also had a great sense of humor. Later on, after Tanya and I were married, he'd come down and stay with us during spring training. Mickey Mantle really liked him. Because of Tony's childhood accident, he looked kind of tangle-eyed, and Mickey would always kid him.

"Tony," he'd say, "you'd make a hell of a traffic cop. You'd be out there pointing this way and that way and all kinds of different ways." Mickey let Tony sit at his locker, and he gave him one of his game-used bats. After Tony's death in the late '60s, his daughter sold it for $7,000. Today, it'd go for around $50,000.

Introducing Tony to Mickey and some of the other Yankees was small payback for how he helped me during those early months of 1960. After the first rejection, I'd submitted my request again—and again, the Army had turned it down. I kept trying, though, in spite of the fact that my company commander told me I wasn't going to make it, that I was stuck. Another colonel—an old warhorse named Sarwark, who hated peacetime—supervised my work at Fort Leonard Wood. He was more encouraging. "Keep trying," he'd tell me. "You'll get out eventually." I overheard several of their conversations on whether or not I'd ever get my early release. I even heard the notion that I was being kept on base because the officer in charge of my release was not a Yankee fan.

For a time, it looked like the company commander was going to be right. Every time I tried, I got sent back to square one. I was beginning to get pissed, especially when I saw the other guys packing up and leaving, like future Dodgers star Ron Perranoski, who was then pitching in the Texas League for San Antonio, the Cubs' Double-A affiliate. We worked out in the gym and played a lot of catch during our time together at Fort Leonard Wood. After getting his early release and going to spring training, he caught on with the Dodgers. In fact, I ran into him again at Vero Beach, Florida, where the Dodgers trained, later that spring. He was in the process then of developing that great sinker and becoming a ground-ball pitcher.

On the other hand, it looked like *I* wasn't going anywhere. My request kept getting rejected, and I developed such a bad attitude that it looked like a court-martial might be in my future. But then Tony Schartz gave me a call, asking me how it was going.

"Not good," I told him. "I'm *stuck* over here. I'm not getting out early, although I'm clearly entitled to it. I'm not asking for anything the other ballplayers aren't asking for, and they're all getting released for spring training."

"All right. Sit tight. I'm going to give our congressman J. Floyd Breeding a call, and he'll get hold of Lyndon Johnson and check out your situation."

Our future president Johnson was then the U.S. Senate Majority Leader. The next thing I knew, the post's adjutant general, a major-general named Lee, had gotten a call from Senator Johnson asking why Private Terry hadn't been released.

As I understand it, Lee told him, "We're letting everyone out who applies for early release. I've got 30 or 40 captains and colonels who are processing the applications, and apparently his just fell into some unfavorable hands. Maybe whoever denied him just doesn't like the Yankees."

"If this man isn't released immediately," Johnson returned, "I want all the records of the six-month athletic personnel on my desk. And if I find any discrepancies, there'll be a full-fledged investigation!"

The very next day, I got a TWX, a military telegram: "Delighted to inform you that you will be released immediately. Senator Lyndon Baines Johnson."

How about *that* for getting action? Almost before I had time to digest the good news, a couple of soldiers came by and told me, "Get your duffel bag. You're outta here." I couldn't oblige them fast enough.

In July of 1960, only a few months after he'd gotten me my early release from the Army via J. Floyd Breeding and Lyndon Johnson, Tony was the highest-ranking Kansas delegate to the Democratic National Convention in Los Angeles when John F. Kennedy got the nomination. Kennedy had lots of real competition that year, including Missouri senator Pat Brown, Senator Hubert Humphrey, former presidential candidate Adlai Stevenson, and Johnson, Kennedy's eventual running mate. At the time, though, Johnson was pushing hard for the top spot.

Kansas sent 22 delegates to the '60 convention. In the first roll call, they voted 11-10 for Kennedy before Tony, voting last, cast his vote for Johnson. That deadlocked things for the delegation.

Tony knew Lyndon, and he really liked him. His boys, Thon and Wade, were real active Young Democrats, and they'd told him before the convention, "Pop, you've got to go with Kennedy." Bobby and Teddy Kennedy had come through Kansas and talked to them, so they were impressed with the whole family.

"Nope," Tony told his sons. "Lyndon's my guy." And he proved it by casting his vote for Johnson at the convention. Once Johnson found out about what Tony had done, he sent his bagman, Bobby Baker, off the floor to talk to Tony.

"Tony," Baker said, "if you keep Kansas deadlocked and we get through the first ballot, it's a free ball—all commitments are off. Then we'll have a chance to win this nomination. Do that, and Lyndon'll give you anything you want."

"All right. I want to be ambassador to Luxembourg," said Tony, referring to the tiny country next to his ancestral home of Germany.

Johnson lost to Kennedy on that first ballot, 806 votes to 409 (with 10 other candidates splitting the rest). Still, after he became president, following Kennedy's assassination, LBJ kept his word. When the ambassador to Luxembourg retired under his watch, Johnson called Tony up and said, "The job's yours if you want it."

Unfortunately, by that time Tony had to decline for health reasons. He'd developed a tumor on his cerebellum. He went to Barnes Hospital in St. Louis, a great hospital, where he was put in a ward with 10 other guys who had a similar problem. Although he'd only last about five more years, he became the only one of them to survive the grueling process of having the tumor shaved off his brain.

But even when he was dealing with something that terrible, Tony kept his sense of humor. The operation was done at Barnes, and after it was over, he told me, "I was operated on by a Jewish doctor and a black surgeon. I am no longer prejudiced."

08

A TEAM OF SUPERSTARS

About the time I started applying for my early release from the military, the Yankees made a deal with the A's, sending Kansas City four good players: my fellow starting pitcher Don Larsen, who'd thrown that World Series perfect game I'd watched from my hospital room in Kansas City three years earlier; Hank Bauer and Norm Siebern, two-thirds of our starting outfielders (Mickey being the other); and backup first baseman Marv Throneberry. Two of the three guys we got in return, Joe DeMaestri and Kent Hadley, were backups, both gone from our roster by '62. The third one was a very different story. In fact, his joining the Yankees was one of the reasons the early '60s team became one of the greatest, if not *the* greatest, offensive baseball clubs of all time.

Roger Maris had come to the Athletics in a trade with the Cleveland Indians about 18 months earlier—supposedly with a proviso from Indians general manager Frank Lane that Maris could not be traded to New York. Lane knew that Roger could pull the ball, so he was tailor-made for Yankee Stadium's short right field porch. The Cleveland GM didn't want to put another big offensive weapon in the team's arsenal; it was hard enough for his team, and all the others in the American League, to beat the Yanks.

If there was such a proviso, though, neither A's GM Parke Carroll nor his Yankees counterpart, George Weiss, paid any attention to it. And the only reason Maris went on the trading block in the first place was because he'd come back too soon from an appendectomy. In the early part of the '59 season, he was tearing up the American League as a Kansas City Athletic, with an average around .340. He was hitting a lot of homers, but he could also bunt and hit the ball to all parts of the field. And he could run. He was George Brett with power.

Then Roger had his appendix taken out, and he tried to return too quickly. He wasn't at full strength, and he ended up getting about five hits in his next 60 at-bats. His batting average dropped into the mid-.200s. Coming back a little bit at the end of the season, he finished with decent numbers—16 homers, 72 RBIs, and a .273 average—but his promise in the first part of the season hadn't really been fulfilled. If he'd been healthy the whole year, I think the Yankees would've had a lot of trouble getting him at any price.

During those few years following the transition of the Kansas City baseball team from a Triple-A Yankee franchise to an American League club in competition with those same Yankees, a lot of fans had the notion that the New York execs were treating Kansas City as though it were still a Yankee farm team. It seemed to them that every time the A's started developing a future star, the Yanks would sweep in and snatch him up, trading however many players it took to get the young phenom to put on pinstripes. And whenever this talk came around, Roger Maris was usually exhibit A.

But as I alluded to in an earlier chapter, the reason for those trades had more to do with the fact that the Kansas City A's were a perennial American League doormat, usually finishing seventh out of eight teams, just above the Senators. Teams like those had a lot of holes to fill, and they'd often trade quality to get quantity. Usually forgotten when people bring the Maris trade up is the main guy on the other side of the deal.

Hank Bauer was 37 years old and near the end of his career, and Larsen and Throneberry were traded to different teams in June of '61—although they'd both been first-string guys on the 1960 A's team—but Norm Siebern hung in there as a starter for Kansas City, first as a left fielder and then as a first baseman. In 1962, he drove in 117 runs for the A's—second in the league to the Twins' future hall of famer Harmon Killebrew—played in all 162 games, and batted .308 with 25 home runs. He was an All-Star in both '62 and '63, and went on to have more good years after being traded to the Orioles for cash and another star, Jim Gentile, after the 1963 season. So despite what it might've looked like to some fans, the A's didn't just give Roger Maris away. Siebern was a legitimate star.

Still, when Stengel put Roger in the lineup back-to-back with Mantle, that ignited our offense. Along with the big trade with Baltimore that brought Turley and Larsen to the Yanks, it was the deal for Maris that really put us in the driver's seat.

* * * *

For the military reasons explained in the last chapter, I made it to spring training a couple weeks late, and I got off to a slow start because I was still getting into shape. After the season started, Casey eased me onto the mound during our fourth game of 1960, where I pitched the final two innings at Yankee Stadium in relief of Whitey Ford, not allowing a run and earning my very first save as a member of the Yankees. (I'd gotten two as a member of the A's staff in '58.)

After one more relief appearance, I made my season debut as a starter on Sunday, May 1, against the Orioles at Memorial Stadium, giving up two runs in the first two innings before Casey pulled me for Bobby Shantz. My next two starts went a lot better: a complete-game, five-hit shutout against my former team, the Kansas City A's, in New York, and another complete home game five days later against Cleveland. I lost 3-2 on an unearned run, but I pitched all 11 innings of that two-hour and 52-minute game.

I had a real good second half and ended up 10-8 with a 3.40 ERA, seven complete games—three of them shutouts—and even a couple of saves. That was nine fewer saves than 34-year-old Shantz, a veteran left-handed starter the Yankees had converted to a relief specialist, who led the team in that department during 1960. For the preceding two seasons, our top reliever had been Ryne Duren, whose 19 saves had led the entire American League in '58. The next year he'd racked up 14, posting great earned-run averages both seasons (2.02 and 1.88, respectively). But he'd slipped in 1960, managing only 8 saves with an ERA more than three runs above his 1959 total.

* * * *

We went to the World Series against the Pittsburgh Pirates at the end of 1960, and when you go to a Series as a ballplayer, you have to get used to people popping out of the woodwork to try to get tickets—especially since all the games were usually sold out. That year, the Series started at Forbes Field, and I was contacted by a car dealer from Lawton, Oklahoma, who was a big Yankee fan and especially a Mickey Mantle fan. He'd driven all the way to Pittsburgh only to find out that he couldn't buy a ticket anywhere. My dad lived in Lawton at the time, and I'd been there to visit, so I knew who the guy was, and I was able to get him two seats in the right field bleachers, right above Roberto Clemente, in the second or third row. In the second game, Mantle—batting right-handed against the lefty Fred Green—hit a line-drive home run to right, practically in this guy's lap. He caught it, and after the game I had Mickey sign it for him. Isn't that something? A guy comes all the way from Lawton, Oklahoma, to see Mickey Mantle in a World Series game, and Mickey hits a homer right to him.

I'd played a little bit of a role in getting Mickey and the rest of us to the Series that year. On September 25, I had started the 149th game of the season for the Yankees in Fenway Park, getting all but the last out (Luis Arroyo came in for that) and winning 4-3, clenching the pennant. After all these years, I can't remember whether or not I gave any thought to how nervous I'd been in that same ballpark back in '56, the first time I'd ever pitched in the majors. I can tell you, though, that I had two hits in that 4-3 pennant-clencher, including a double, and I drove in a run.

The first action I saw against the Pirates in the Series came in the fourth game. Casey started me against Vern Law, who'd already won the first game of the Series. Law had not only led the Pirates staff with 20 wins during the regular season; he'd also led all the majors with 18 complete games (sharing that honor with the great Milwaukee Braves tandem of Warren Spahn and Lew Burdette). To top off his big year, he won the Cy Young Award, which then was only given to a single pitcher instead of one from each league. By that standard, he was the best hurler in the majors in 1960.

I held my own against him, pitching a pretty good six innings on our home turf but losing 3-2. Two of the worst calls I've ever seen in all my years in baseball didn't help.

The first one came in the very first inning. With the bases loaded and one out, Yogi came up and hit one of Law's pitches off the end of his bat. Because Yogi was a left-handed pull hitter, Don Hoak, the Pirates' third baseman, was shifted toward short, so he grabbed Yogi's grounder, stepped on third, and threw to first. But Yogi was fast, and before the ball got to their first baseman, Dick Stuart, Yogi had stepped on the bag. In fact, he was coming down with his *second* step when Stuart caught the ball. Yogi was clearly safe—there's replay footage out there that proves it beyond a doubt— but the first-base ump, who was a National Leaguer, called him out. We had a big inning going, and because of that call, we only got one run out of it.

Before that, it looked like we were going to break the game open. Did the fact that we'd blown them out the previous two games, 16-3 and 10-0, have anything to do with the bad call from a National League umpire? That's a pretty good question.

Then, in the fifth inning, their right-handed hitting left fielder, Gino Cimoli, hit a ground ball between first and second for a single. Next up was their catcher, Smokey Burgess, and he hit a big hopper to Moose at first. It looked like a double-play ball, but it stuck in Skowron's glove and he was slow getting it out, so he could only go for the force at second. He threw to shortstop Tony Kubek, who was stretched out to take it at second, and Cimoli was out by a mile. But the third-base umpire, Johnny Stevens—who was, I have to say, from the American League—called him safe.

I got the next two guys, Hoak and Mazeroski, on popups, but then Law came up and hit a double to left field, and Bill Virdon, their center-fielder and leadoff hitter, followed him with a bloop single to center, and all of a sudden we were down 3-1 on a pair of terrible calls.

For all that, Moose Skowron almost won the game for us. He had a solo homer in the fourth and scored again on a Bobby Richardson ground-out in the seventh, after knocking one of Law's offerings into the rightfield stands for a ground-rule double. But it wasn't quite enough, and by the time I pitched in the series again, each team had won three games. In our three wins, we'd blown them out by scores of 16-3, 10-0, and 12-0, while their wins had been by much smaller margins.

We all know that none of that really matters in baseball, and it didn't matter then. We were going to Game Seven, and I would end up on the field at the end of the game, following one of the most famous home runs in World Series history.

* * * *

The first time I recall hearing the question was in spring training the next year, when all the writers seemed to want to know the same thing: Did the traumatic experience you had in Game Seven warp you psychologically?

I'll say now what I said then. "Hell, no. Why should it? It was a great thrill just to be *in* my first World Series. I'm looking forward to getting into another one."

That was the truth. It's what I told anyone else who asked—and a lot of people did, especially before and during the 1961 season. Back then, the minimum major league salary was $6,000, so we needed the extra money the Series brought each of us. We really did. You got into the World Series, and the first couple of games you were just happy to be there. Then you started getting mad at one another and things turned competitive in a hurry.

I was lucky enough to get into *several* more Series, including another one that found me on the mound at the end of Game Seven—and turned out a lot better from my point of view. But first, a little bit of insight into what happened that Thursday, October 13, 1960, at Forbes Field in Pittsburgh.

First of all, I want to tell you something I learned early on, even before my time as a professional ballplayer: *You* have to be the judge, the honest judge, of your own performance. Sometimes you pitch lousy, but you win. Other times, you pitch really well and lose. You've always got to be really honest when you appraise one of your performances. *You've* got to be the one, because you're the only one who knows everything about it. It happened to *you*. You can't depend on what fans say, because they can't know exactly what's happened and what was involved. For instance, if you're up in the stands and you see a seemingly routine ground ball glance off the shortstop's body for an error, you'll probably think it was just a bad play on his part. There's no way for you to know that the ball hit a little pebble on the field and took a funny bounce. He can't hold up a sign that says, "BALL HIT A PEBBLE." So you've got to be judge, jury, and sometimes executioner of your own performance.

Breaking into the big leagues is tough, and a lot of times I was my own worst critic. From the beginning, as I moved up the ladder, I didn't necessarily want to be a *star*, but I didn't want to be a part-time player or a role player. I wanted to be a regular, take my turn in the rotation every few days, and make my contribution to a team. So I had to learn to evaluate what I'd done and try to figure out what changes I needed to make to get better. I also had to learn how to deal with giving my best and losing anyway.

It wasn't easy to lose, though, when you were a New York Yankee. Every time we lost a game, you could hear a pin drop in the clubhouse. It was very serious business to both players and fans—especially to the players. When I finally began pitching regularly for New York, I left my room at the Commodore Hotel for an apartment on 85th Street and Park Avenue, a fourth-floor brownstone walkup. After a game in which I hadn't pitched well, I'd often end up pacing the streets of Manhattan until very early in the morning, watching the steam come out around the manhole covers, riding the subway to Brooklyn and back with derelicts and a handful of drunks as my only companions. Usually, it took a long time for me to shed that game face and get over a bad performance.

One time while I was still with the Kansas City A's, I was taking a loss real hard, and Tom Gorman, an old pitcher, said, "Ralph, the sun's gonna come up tomorrow, whether you won the game or lost it."

The next day, he came over to me. "Did the sun come up today?" he asked.

"Go to hell, Tom," I answered.

But I did eventually learn how to deal with losing. You have to, or you could end up like the Angels' Donnie Moore, who never got over giving up the 11th inning run in the fifth game of the 1986 American League Championship Series that handed the Red Sox the pennant, or Hugh Casey, the pitcher in that infamous World Series game of 1941 between the Yankees and the Dodgers, after Mickey Owen missed the potentially game-ending third strike and the Yankees came back to take the series. Although there were other factors involved, both of those guys ended up dying by their own hands.

If you're reading this book, I'm figuring you know what happened between Bill Mazeroski and me during Game Seven at Forbes Field. The score had been seesawing back and forth since the bottom of the first, when their first baseman, Rocky Nelson, hit a two-run homer off Turley. By the time I got into the game, in the bottom of the eighth, Casey had used four pitchers and Danny Murtaugh, his counterpart, had used three.

I warmed up five different times before I finally took the mound, in relief of Jim Coates, who'd just given up a single to Clemente and a home run to the Pirates' catcher, Hal Smith. I retired Don Hoak on a fly to left, getting us out of the eighth inning. Down 9-7, we rallied in the top of the ninth with singles by Richardson and pinch-hitter Dale Long, and they both scored, Richardson on a Mantle single and Long on a groundout by Yogi. So when I came back out to the mound, we were knotted up at 9-9.

Although I'd been able to get Hoak, I wasn't at all in a groove. The pitching mound at the side of Forbes Field where I'd been warming up was small and steep, but the mound on the diamond itself was high and flat. I wasn't making the necessary adjustment. My foot was hitting too early, and everything was going high. I threw a couple of extra warmup pitches to try and adjust, but I still couldn't get the ball down. I even tried to bounce it in, and I couldn't.

Elston had been hit on the hand by a Bob Friend pitch during his first at-bat in Game Six, so he wasn't available to catch. Yogi was in left field that day. So my catcher was Johnny Blanchard. He knew immediately that I had a problem. After I took my warmup tosses, he came out to the mound and said, "Ralph. You've got to get the ball down."

"Yeah, yeah, I know," I told him. "I will."

First up for the Pirates in the bottom of the ninth was their No. 8 hitter and second baseman, Bill Mazeroski. Despite my best effort, I was high with my first pitch to him, which went in for a ball, and high with the second as well, which went over the left-field wall. Game over. The Pirates won 10-9 on what is still the only World Series ever decided by a Game Seven home run. It was also the only time I ever saw Mickey Mantle cry.

As the Forbes Field crowd went crazy in the stands, I left the mound and walked through the dugout into the visitors' clubhouse and sat down. In a little bit, the clubhouse guy came over.

"You want something to drink?" he asked.

As I've said, I wasn't much of a drinker. But I told him, "Yeah. I could go for a Schlitz."

"We don't have Schlitz," he said. "We've got Iron City and Hudepohl."

I hadn't heard of either one of those brands.

"Okay. Bring me a Hudepohl."

I sat there and drank my Hudepohl, and then I went in to the office to see Casey. I not only felt bad about the game, I felt bad about Casey, because we all had the feeling that he'd said goodbye to us in the meeting we'd had earlier.

Casey's clubhouse meetings were usually classic. He had that gravelly bourbon voice, and he'd say stuff like, "You damn guys got to start playing better, or the moving van's pulling up in front of your house and you're going to be *traded* to *Kansas City.*" That was the ultimate threat. I couldn't keep from laughing whenever he said that— even when I was one of the few guys in the meeting who'd actually *been* traded to Kansas City.

Casey's meetings affected Mickey the same way they affected me. When Casey really got going, Mickey and I were afraid to look at each other for fear of busting out with the church-house giggles. Mickey would be choking back laughter, and I'd be trying desperately to keep a straight face.

Casey would also mispronounce names, which was another great source of amusement. He'd say, "Well, Kaleen and Koon up there in Detroit, how are we gonna pitch to 'em, Jim?" He meant Al Kaline and Harvey Kuenn, but our pitching coach, Jim Turner, wouldn't ever correct him.

"We've got to pitch Kaleen this way," he'd say, "and Koon that way."

The meeting before Game Seven, though, wasn't funny at all. All Casey did was call us all together and tell us, "Boys, it's been a great year, and when the Series is over, I'll have to go on TV with Murtaugh and congratulate him, or he'll congratulate me. However it goes, you've done a fine job. Have a good winter."

We'd all heard the rumors that Casey was being let go after the Series, and it turned out to be true. There was lots of speculation about why he was dismissed, including his advancing age. Later, Casey addressed that rumor indirectly when he said, "I'll never make the mistake of being 70 again."

For whatever reason, Casey Stengel would never manage another game in pinstripes, and when I went into his office after Game Seven, I was pretty sure it was the last time I'd ever be having a player-to-manager conversation with him.

Casey was sitting back in the chair behind his desk, his jersey unbuttoned halfway, his pants down around his shoes. He was taking off his Yankee uniform for what would be the last time. Later on, I would think about what a rare moment that was.

"What's up, kid?" he said.

"Case, I feel bad, ending it for you this way."

"How were you trying to pitch him?" he asked.

"I knew he was a high-fastball hitter," I said. "I was trying to give him breaking stuff, and I couldn't get the ball down."

"Well," Casey said, "you're not always going to get the ball where you want to. That's a *physical* mistake, not a *mental* mistake. Anyone can make a physical mistake. As long as you didn't go against the scouting report—if you had, I wouldn't sleep good at night."

"I didn't. I knew how I wanted to pitch him. I just couldn't get the ball down."

"Okay," he said. "Forget it, kid. Come back and have a good year next year."

He could've hung a guilt trip on me. But he didn't. That was just another reason I will always love Casey Stengel.

* * * *

As I wrote earlier, Tanya had come to see me when I was at Fort Leonard Wood, and that's when we finally knew we were serious about one another and this was it for both of us. So in early 1960, not quite two years after we'd met in the corner of old Municipal Stadium in Kansas City, we got engaged.

A little later on, after the season had started, I went in to see Casey.

"Tanya and I would like to get married over the All-Star Game break," I told him.

He just about choked. "Well, uh, uh—why don't you wait until the season's over?" I wasn't sure why he was acting that way until I realized that he figured my getting married might be a distraction and affect my performance on the mound.

"If you wait," he continued, "maybe somebody'll give you a trip to Europe."

"Yeah," I said, "and maybe not. They give trips to Mickey and Yogi and people like that, but who the hell's going to give *me* a trip?"

"Well, I think you should wait."

So we did. We waited until the season and the World Series were both over, and we set the date for the first weekend of November 1960. But we'd failed to take into consideration how big a deal pheasant hunting is in Kansas, where all Tanya's relatives lived. When word got out about our proposed wedding date, they all told us, "You can't do *that*. November's the opening of *pheasant season*." So we delayed it another week and got married in Kansas City on November 12.

Tanya's Catholic, and I was a Baptist, so I had to take instructions. They were given me by a Jesuit priest, Father Hogan, at Saint Ignatius Loyola Church in New York. Then we went to the Cathedral of the Immaculate Conception in downtown Kansas City to be married. After the ceremony, we went on our honeymoon to Acapulco and stayed at Las Brisas, a famous hotel on the beach. One day we saw some people out there kicking a football around, and when I went down to check things out, I saw that it was Bobby, Ethel, and Ted Kennedy. So I started kicking the ball around with them, told them about Tanya's Uncle Tony, and congratulated them on John Kennedy's recent election to the highest office in America. I meant it, too. I thought Kennedy was something special. He'd served in the military, and he had real leadership qualities.

As it turned out, the reason his family members were down there was to celebrate his victory. And I'm telling you, what nice people.

Of course, they were famous. But I found out I was kind of famous, too—even in Acapulco. Someone from the local paper found out Tanya and I were there, and when I picked up the sports page one day, I saw my name in the headline. As I remember it, part of it read, "RALPH TERRY y MAZEROSKI."

I was in another country, on my honeymoon, and I *still* couldn't get away from Game Seven. Standing there scanning that foreign sports page, I came to the understanding, maybe for the first time, that baseball lore would forever link Mazeroski and me.

09

THE HITTING SEASON

Through the years, I've had people ask me if I thought the 1961 Yankees team was the greatest one ever. I tend to agree with something Mickey once said: "It might've not been the best team of all time, but I can't think of one better."

The one it's usually compared with is the famed 1927 squad, with its Murderer's Row anchored by Ruth and Gehrig and stocked with players like Bob Meusel, Earle Combs, and Tony Lazzeri, all of whom made big contributions with their bats. The '27 Yankees had a great pitching staff, too, with 22-game winner Waite Hoyt the top guy, along with Urban Shocker, who went 18-6; Wilcy Moore, who won 19, mostly coming out of the bullpen, and the lefty Herb Pennock, who was 19-8.

How did we stack up against those legends? Well, it's hard to compare greatness, and you don't win many arguments when you're talking baseball anyway. But I could make a good case that, at least as a *hitting* team, the 1961 Yanks were the best of all time. For one thing, our squad hit 240 home runs (vs. 158 for the '27 Yankees), which was the most in major league history before the advent of the designated hitter. We had two guys, Mantle and Maris, chasing Ruth's record of 60 homers, which he'd set in 1927—and one of them caught and surpassed the Babe that year.

Just the catching staff—Yogi, Elston Howard, and Johnny Blanchard—had 64 homers, a lot of them pinch-hits.

And we had the top three percentage pitchers in the American League: Whitey was 25-4, I was 16-3, and Luis Arroyo was 15-5 with 29 saves; he'd had to go as many as three innings to get some of them. Bill Stafford, who went 14-9, had a 2.68 ERA, which ended up second in the league. The White Sox threw Dick Donovan in for a couple of innings on a Sunday right at the end of the season, and he beat Stafford for the title by a few percentage points.

Thursday, October 13, 1960 at Forbes Field

NEW YORK YANKEES	ab	r	h	rbi	PITTSBURGH PIRATES	ab	r	h	rbi
Richardson 2b	5	2	2	0	Virdon cf	4	1	2	2
Kubek ss	3	1	0	0	Groat ss	4	1	1	1
DeMaestri ss	0	0	0	0	Skinner lf	2	1	0	0
Long ph	1	0	1	0	Nelson 1b	3	1	1	2
McDougald pr, 3b	0	1	0	0	Clemente rf	4	1	1	1
Maris rf	5	0	0	0	Burgess c	3	0	2	0
Mantle cf	5	1	3	2	Christopher pr	0	0	0	0
Berra lf	4	2	1	4	Smith c	1	1	1	3
Skowron 1b	5	2	2	1	Hoak 3b	3	1	0	0
Blanchard c	4	0	1	1	Mazeroski 2b	4	2	2	1
Boyer 3b, ss	4	0	1	1	Law p	2	0	0	0
Turley p	0	0	0	0	Face p	0	0	0	0
Stafford p	0	0	0	0	Cimoli ph	1	1	1	0
Lopez ph	1	0	1	0	Friend p	0	0	0	0
Shantz p	3	0	1	0	Haddix p	0	0	0	0
Coates p	0	0	0	0					
Terry p	0	0	0	0					
Totals	40	9	13	9	Totals	31	10	11	10

```
NEW YORK     0 0 0   0 1 4   0 2 2 – 9  13  1
PITTSBURGH   2 2 0   0 0 0   0 5 1 –10  11  0
```

Mickey and Maris – the home-run hitting M&M Boys.

Stafford, by the way, was a hell of a pitcher. I thought he was one of the best-looking right-handers I ever saw. A couple of years later, in 1963, he was pitching for us in the second game of the season on a chilly day in Kansas City. He threw three-quarters overhand, and he got up on top with a rising fastball to a left-handed hitter named Billy Bryan, one of the A's catchers. I was in the dugout, and I heard a sickening snapping noise and Stafford hollering "Owwwww!" like he'd been hit. They didn't know a lot about rotator cuff injuries then, and Stafford was never the same pitcher after that, although he stuck around for a few years—ending his career, ironically, with the Kansas City A's. But boy, he was a good one before his shoulder injury.

Our fourth starter was a rookie, Rollie Sheldon. He was pretty good, too, going 11-5. Bud Daley, Bob Turley, and Jim Coates also got some starts. We ended up winning 109 games, one fewer than that 1927 group.

I'm not about to tell you I think we were better than the 1927 Yankees. What I will say is that in 1961, after the Yankees traded for Maris in '60 and put him back-to-back with Mickey, new manager Ralph Houk inherited one of the best teams ever. We were loaded, and Maris had a lot to do with it. In fact, we won five straight pennants with him on our side, and he won two MVP Awards during that time, which meant he was a dominant player in his era—pretty good for a guy who's not in the Baseball Hall of Fame.

* * * *

As I think about that 1927 squad and our 1961 version of the Yankees, I remember an old-timer's game at Yankee Stadium, which I believe was held in '61. Thirty-four years separated those two teams, and while guys like Meusel, Combs, and Waite Hoyt were still around, many of the '27 stars had already passed on by that time, including Ruth. His wife Claire, however, maintained a relationship with the club and showed up for a lot of events.

I remember our great PA announcer, Bob Sheppard, calling her name that day. Mrs. Ruth was in the owner's box, up in the mezzanine, waving to the fans and looking as though she might have knocked back a few adult beverages. After the game, I was talking to Merlin and Carmen, Mickey's wife and Yogi's wife, and someone brought up Babe's wife.

"One of these days," I told them, "that'll be you guys up in the boxes, waving to the fans like Mrs. Babe Ruth."

"Oh, no," they said. "We'll never be *that* old."

Claire Ruth was somewhere around 65 at the time.

BABE RUTH, THE GREAT BAMBINO

* * * *

I had a good year in '61. On the home front, our first son, Raif Galen Terry—his middle name a tribute to my best friend from Chelsea High, Galen Hudspeth—was born at Lenox Hill Hospital in Manhattan. Baseball-wise, I had a 3.15 ERA to go with my 16 wins, and the Yankees headed again to the World Series, winning four games to one against the Cincinnati Reds. I started Game Two and Game Five, losing the first one and getting a no-decision in the fifth, which was won by Bud Daley in relief. We had a terrific season, but everything else we did was overshadowed that year because of the pursuit of Babe Ruth's regular-season home-run record by a pair of Yankee sluggers the press and fans dubbed the M&M boys, Roger Maris and Mickey Mantle.

I don't imagine I need to tell you how it turned out, but for the record, Mickey ended up with 54 and Roger with 61—a new record and, as many still believe, an "asterisk" in the record books.

Nineteen-sixty-one was the first year the American League expanded its number of games from 154, which had stood since 1920, to 162. (The National League would follow a year later.) And, as Maris and Mantle began closing in on the Babe, Ford Frick, the Commissioner of Major League Baseball—and a former newspaperman who happened to be Babe Ruth's good friend and ghostwriter—publicly declared that if anyone was to break Ruth's record that year, he would have to do it in the same number of games Ruth played. That, of course, was 154. Otherwise, Frick said, something would have to be done in the record books—"some distinctive mark"—to indicate the new record took more games to set than Ruth's.

So when Maris did break Ruth's mark by one, it went down in the record books with one of the most famous asterisks in history. Or so the story goes. In fact, major league baseball didn't even have an official record book at the time, and no others that I knew of used an asterisk in their listings of Maris's single-season home-run record. The whole "asterisk" thing got started at the news conference Frick held on July 17 of '61 to make his declaration. Sportswriter Dick Young, who was with the *New York Daily News* at the time, suggested a new record set in more than 154 games should have an asterisk, which was often used to show "a difference of opinion."

Still, the legend persists. And if there was indeed an "asterisk game," which would've been the last game Maris could've gotten the record in the same number of games as Ruth, I pitched all nine innings of it, squaring off against the Baltimore Orioles' Milt Pappas.

It was the 154th game of the season. We played it on September 20th at Memorial Stadium in Baltimore and won 4-2, clinching the American League pennant. Roger hit his 59th homer of the season in the third inning, but because we were now over the 154-game threshold, we knew that Frick would not consider Roger the new single-season record-holder for home runs even if he did beat Ruth's 60.

(A lot of people don't remember that Roger's home run that night would've tied Ruth's record if he, Roger, hadn't had a homer erased earlier in the year. He'd hit one against the Indians at Cleveland Municipal Stadium, but the game was called on account of rain after four innings, so it didn't count.)

I remember the first time Maris came up the night we clinched. The wind was blowing in about 18 miles an hour from right center, and he hit a shot off Pappas, a low fastball, that right-fielder Earl Robinson caught up against the fence. I'll give Pappas credit: He didn't pitch around Roger. He challenged him.

The second time up, in the third inning, Roger hit another one, and this time Robinson didn't catch it. I mean, Roger nailed it—about 380 feet, right in the teeth of that wind. Gone.

Then, his third time up, he hit one into the stands that almost became No. 60, hooking about three feet to the side of the foul pole in right. But that was it. When he came up for the last time, knuckleballer Hoyt Wilhelm was on the mound, and Roger tried to check his swing on one of those knucklers but dribbled it back to Wilhelm instead.

A lot has been written about Roger and that 1961 season, and some have suggested that he and Mickey didn't get along. That's all bullshit. They had no problems at all. Roger's dad was an old Frisco railroad man, and Roger was raised to be strong and tough. He'd dive into the bleachers to make a catch, knowing that the right-field wall in Yankee Stadium was made of concrete. He'd go hard into second base. But he was also a good guy, a quiet guy, who was under an unbelievable amount of pressure during that '61 season. People think that they didn't have the media then that they have now, but that's wrong. There were more newspapers, more reporters, and no cooling-off period for a player. The minute the game was over, they'd be right on top of Roger, stacked 15 deep in front of his locker.

"What pitch did you hit?"

"Did you know it was gone when you hit it?"

"You think you're going to break the record?"

"What did you have for breakfast?"

"Did you sleep well last night?"

It was the same old shit every day. But he put up with it. He was very patient with everyone—but you only crossed him once, and that was it. You wouldn't get a second chance. A good example of that was what happened between Roger and a friend of mine, the sportswriter Oscar Fraley.

Fraley was a little guy who looked like Don Knotts. He even had a vein that would throb in his forehead whenever he got agitated. He was also a big-time writer. He wrote a lot of books and tons of newspaper stuff, first for Associated Press, and then with United Press International. He'd co-authored the 1957 nonfiction book *The Untouchables* along with famed G-Man Elliot Ness, which became the basis for the popular TV series of the same name featuring Robert Stack playing Ness. Fraley's newspaper work including a long-running UPI column called "Fearless Fraley Predicts," in which he would make predictions about the scores of upcoming football games, or give his thoughts in the preseason about what the baseball standings would be at the end of the year. He covered heavyweight fights, the Olympics, everything.

I used to hang out and play golf with Fraley, and one time he told me about covering the 1956 Olympics in Melbourne, Australia, right during the height of the Cold War. He said the U.S. got screwed that year—a

Russian would make a dive, and the judges would give him a 10, and an American would make a dive that was just as good and get a two.

In 1962, our spring training camp opened in a brand-new facility in Fort Lauderdale, Florida, on the opposite coast and about 250 miles south of St. Petersburg, our old training site. In those days, most of the sports reporters for the major papers and wire services would come around and spend some time in each major league camp. I believe it was just after St. Patrick's Day when they visited us, and I was good friends with a few of them, like Milton Richman, a nice old guy who was a top writer for UPI; UPI editor Leo Petersen; and Fraley, who was also with UPI then.

Everything ran on schedule in spring training, so when it was your time to get in the batting cage, you had to be there and ready. Of course, after the 1961 season, Roger had become the focus of a lot of attention, so while others were standing around the cage waiting to take their swings, he was beside our dugout, signing autographs for people in the stands. That day, there was some grandmother there with a little kid, and just as they approached Roger, he got called to the batting cage.

"I gotta go," he said. "I've got to get in the cage." And he left without signing an autograph for the kid.

Oscar was sitting there watching, and maybe it's because he was a little hungover from celebrating St. Patrick's Day and not in a good mood, but he wrote this *ripper* article about Roger. It talked about how Roger wouldn't sign an autograph for the boy and added something like, "When my son grows up, I don't want him to be like Roger Maris. I want him to be like John Glenn"—who had just become the first person to circle the earth. It was really a vicious story.

A couple of days after Oscar's story ran, the writers were still around, and Roger asked Joe Trimble, the sportswriter for the *New York Daily News*, if he knew Oscar Fraley.

"Sure," Trimble said, and pointed him out.

Roger made a beeline to him. "Who are you, you little son of a bitch?" he asked Fraley. "What rock did you crawl out from under? I've never even *met* you. I don't know who in the hell you are. How could you write that garbage about me? You don't even *know* me."

"Well," Oscar said, "let's talk about it."

"There ain't gonna *be* no talking," Roger said, and turned away. It was a cold day, and as Roger stalked away, Joe Trimble said, loud enough for everyone else to hear, "See, Oscar, I *told* you that you shouldn't have asked if you could use his windbreaker."

In the wake of the story, all the other big sports reporters felt like they had gotten scooped. They started asking Roger about what had happened, and he got turned off and stopped granting any print interviews. So then some of the writers started manufacturing stuff: Roger Maris was a crybaby. His own teammates didn't like him. It went on for a long time, and it was just not true.

I mean, how could you *not* like the guy? He was playing all out, and doing it all for us. It was vicious and rotten, and I think it has to do with why Roger Maris isn't in the Baseball Hall of Fame. The writers are the ones who vote you in when you become eligible, and they didn't put him in. Then, in later years, his nomination went to the old-timers' committee, and I think it was deadlocked, three for and three against. It's like the Democrats and Republicans. They have separate agendas, and they'd deadlock, so no one would get in. Then they began looking up Negro League stats and bringing up umpires and sportswriters, just so they'd have someone they could agree on to put in the Hall of Fame and justify their own existence.

Roger Maris held the record for single-season home runs for 37 years, four years longer than Ruth held it. In the subsequent years, the ball was souped up, ballpark fences were shortened everywhere except the old parks, Wrigley and Fenway, and *still* nobody hit more home runs than

Roger Maris in 1961, after hitting his 61st home run to break Babe Ruth's long-standing record.

Roger. No one beat his one-season total until the era of performance-enhancing drugs. As I mentioned earlier, Roger was a two-time MVP, in '60 and '61, and played on five pennant-winning Yankee teams, along with a couple more later on when he was with the St. Louis Cardinals. And yet he's not in the Hall of Fame.

I think that's one of baseball's greatest tragedies.

* * * *

After starting golfing as therapy after my car accident in 1957, I quickly got to where I enjoyed it a lot, and I got pretty good at it in a relatively short period of time. I remember in June of that year, just a few months after I'd first picked up the clubs on a regular basis, I shot a 74.

So even after I was fully healed, I kept playing golf whenever I had the opportunity. And in the spring of 1961, just before that great Yankees season, I got the chance to go to work for probably the greatest golfer of our time, Arnold Palmer, who at the time owned ten percent of the Country Club of Miami.

I asked Oscar Fraley, the same sportswriter who'd get into the scrap with Roger later on, to set up a meeting, and Tanya and I went down from camp and met with Arnie and his wife, Winnie, at his club in North Miami.

There, I laid it out for him. "Arnie," I said, "I'd like to work for you in the off-season." Baseball's off-season, wintertime, is the prime golf season in Florida, so that would have worked out perfectly for me. "I can shoot low seventies once in a while, if I make a couple of long putts. I can't play baseball forever, so I'd like to work for you and learn the game."

He said, "Ralph, you come to work for me, and I'll teach you everything I know about golf—my way, because I don't know anybody else's way—and I've got a little condo where you can stay. I want you to work five days a week, but I want you to play every day with the members. If you work in the morning, you play in the afternoon. If you work in the afternoon, play in the morning. I don't think it's right to take a young golfer and stick him behind a counter all day during his best years. You should be playing."

I believe he offered me $400 a month plus the use of the condo, which was just fine with me.

"Okay," I said. "See you when the season's over."

Well, we all know how that year turned out. It helped a lot of us on the Yankees get to that next level in our careers. Also, near the end of the season, our first boy, Raif Galen Terry, was born. So I called Arnie and said, "I've got to take a rain check. My baseball career's picking up, and our first son has just come along."

"All right," he said. "Let me know whenever you need a job."

Since there was only a brief period in which Arnie was in the position to hire me, I never worked for him. But in the latter part of my sports career, after I'd traded the diamond for the links, he became a very good friend, as well as a mentor of mine.

ARNOLD PALMER

* * * *

As you can tell, Casey Stengel was a good friend and mentor as well, right from the beginning. Somewhere around the time I met with Arnie, Casey called me into his office. I didn't know why; I thought maybe I'd done something wrong.

"Terry," he began. He called all of us except for Yogi and Hank Bauer by their last names. "You're a golfer. You play a lot of golf. What do you think about this? I'm looking at investing in a golf project. All putting greens."

"Uh-huh."

"You look at golf on TV," he continued, "and there's Sam Snead hitting 260 yards with a driver, and he hits the left rough, 30 feet from the hole, and then they show a diagram with a line to where he hit it. Then he hits, say, an eight-iron to the green. And here comes Ben Hogan, hitting it 250 yards into the right rough, 25 feet from the hole, and they show *that* diagram. So now here they are, both putting for their birdie threes."

He looked at me. "All it is really is a putting contest. So I'm thinking about building eighteen holes, all greens, and having putting championships. What do you think?"

"Well," I said, "it sounds like a great idea to me."

That's all he wanted me for, just to run that idea by me. I don't know if he ever invested, but courses that were all greens, where they held putting contests, came along later and were popular for a while.

* * * *

One of my most vivid memories from those days is of riding passenger trains, with the old Pullman cars, back when the teams traveled by rail. It seemed like we were always going through Wheeling, West Virginia, at about 4 a.m. You'd sleep a while, and you'd get up and go through the club car, and there'd be Casey, holding court with the writers and reporters. He was a great storyteller, and he could drink 'em all under the table, too.

A while back, I was talking to Tony Kubek, and he said, "Ralph, everybody wants to romanticize that era, but it was hard work. You'd play Cleveland, and then you'd have the White Sox coming up, then you'd have to go to play Boston at Fenway."

It was hard work, but it was fun, too, and easy to romanticize because of all the larger-than-life figures then: Casey, of course, and Whitey and Mickey, who liked to get off the train, have a redcap haul their bags for them, and then ask the man, "You got change for a quarter?"

On July 8, 1958, Mickey and Casey were called by Senator Estes Kefauver to a Senate subcommittee hearing on baseball's anti-trust exemption and the reserve clause that could bind a player to one team for his whole career. It was a big witch hunt, much ado about nothing, and when Casey's time came to testify, he entertained the group with the kind of free-association double-talk that came to be known as Stengelese. Thanks to the online version of *Baseball Almanac* (www.baseball-almanac.com), anyone can see a complete transcript of Casey's testimony, which ranges from his commentary on contemporary players to his observation that Japanese baseballers are handicapped because their hands are smaller.

Here's a sample of that transcription:

Casey: If I am going to go on the road and we are a traveling ball club and you know the cost of transportation now—we travel sometimes with three Pullman coaches, the New York Yankees and remember I am just a salaried man and do not own stock in the New York Yankees, I found out that in traveling with the New York Yankees on the road and all, that it is the best, and we have broken records in Washington this year, we have broken them in every city but New York and we have lost two clubs that have gone out of the city of New York.

Of course, we have had some bad weather, I would say that they are mad at us in Chicago, we fill the parks. They have come out to see good material. I will say they are mad at us in Kansas City, but we broke their attendance record.

Now on the road we only get possibly 27¢. I am not positive of these figures, as I am not an official. If you go back fifteen years or if I owned stock in the club I would give them to you.

Senator Kefauver: Mr. Stengel, I am not sure that I made my question clear.

Casey: Yes, sir. Well that is all right. I am not sure I am going to answer yours perfectly either.

After Casey had held forth along these lines for quite some time, with Kefaufer and several other senators quizzing him, he was dismissed and Kefauver turned to Mickey.

"Mr. Mantle," he asked, "do you have any observations with reference to the applicability of the antitrust laws to baseball?"

"My views are about the same as Casey's," Mickey said.

* * * *

The last two semesters I went to college came after the 1958 seasons, when I attended classes at the University of Kansas City, now known as the University of Missouri at Kansas City. Casey was an alumnus of the same campus, having attended Western Dental College there. (He used to say he never went into dentistry because they didn't make left-handed dental tools.) A Kansas City guy through and through—Charles Dillon Stengel was not only born there, but also got his nickname from the initials K.C., for Kansas City—he knew a lot of people in that town. One of them was a Chevrolet dealer named Dave Sight; the two of them had grown up together. Mr. Sight had been one of the original Chevy dealers in town, with his dealership dating back to the early '20s

I was still with the A's, and I needed a job in the off-season, so Casey told me to go see his friend Dave Sight. I did, and he put me on as a salesman right away, giving me a demo to drive. I think I got $400 a month and a commission for every car I sold.

One day while I was the only guy manning the showroom, these two Middle Eastern guys, small guys, walked in, very neatly dressed in brown suits. They came over and introduced themselves as the Shah of Iran and his trade minister—and they wanted to buy 50 General Motors trucks and have them shipped to their home country. It was too big of a deal for me to handle,

Well before his time as a major league pitcher ended, Ralph had become a formidable golfer.

so I quickly got hold of the sales manager, and he made a deal with them to get the trucks directly from the General Motors plant in Kansas City.

I remember that the Shah spoke perfect English, and he couldn't have been nicer to me. I thought it was kind of neat to be selling something directly to the Shah of Iran.

While I was selling cars for Sight Brothers, I was also going to school at the University of Kansas City. A couple of my instructors, sociology professor Dr. Neil Warshay and psychology professor Dr. Bob Neal, were huge baseball fans and cut me a lot of slack in class because I was a pro ballplayer. They especially hoped one day to meet Casey, one of UKC's most famous former students.

In 1960, after I was back with the Yankees, we were coming into Kansas City to play the A's early in the season, and I told Casey about my two professors.

"They're big baseball fans," I said, "and they'd love to meet you, especially since you're one of their grads."

"Okay," Casey told me. "Have them meet me up at the clubhouse about 4:30, before batting practice." The visitor's clubhouse at Municipal Stadium was over behind third base.

So I got hold of the two professors, and we met before going in to see Casey. As it turned out, Dr. Warshay had put together a lineup he thought Casey might want to see. The major difference was that he had Mickey batting second instead of third, which was his usual spot. The idea was that maybe he'd get an extra at-bat that way. Gil McDougald, our usual second-place hitter at the time, dropped to seventh in Dr. Warshay's scheme. The rest of his lineup was fairly orthodox.

We went in, and Casey regaled us with tales of the old days for a while. Then, I said to Casey, "Case, Neil here's got a lineup that he thinks you ought to use." Only Casey could see my face, and I rolled my eyes as I spoke.

"Is that right?" he asked. "Well, let's see what you've got there, Neil."

Dr. Warshay reached in his pocket and pulled out this little slip of paper like it was the secret to the atomic bomb. He passed it on to Casey, who studied it for a few moments.

"Say, that's a great lineup," he said. "I'll use it tonight."

He did, too. In fact, he had Mickey batting second not only for our two games in Municipal Stadium, but also against the Tigers and Orioles and Senators. And even though Mickey started out in his new spot going 0 for 18, Casey didn't move him back down to third for good until early June.

A relaxed Ralph, early in his career.

Yankees players Elston Howard, Ralph, and Tom Tresh.

Ralph Terry waits in the Yankees dugout during a rain delay in the fifth game of the World Series against the San Francisco Giants. Yankee Stadium, October 9, 1962

Oklahoma Sports Hall of Fame Induction, 2015

Ralph and
Chi-Chi Rodriguez

Yogi Berra and Ralph

Ralph with fellow Oklahoman
and Yankees pitching great
Allie "Superchief" Reynolds

Ralph being interviewed by famed broadcaster Howard Cosell.

Ralph and best friend Cliff Richey

Home-run swings from Yankee sluggers
Maris (above) and Mantle (right).

10

WORLD SERIES REDEMPTION

Although the regular 1962 season may have lacked the headline-grabbing drama of teammates Mickey and Roger chasing the home run record of another famous Yankee, that year's team was a lot like the one before it, the New York squad a lot of baseball fans point to when the subject of all-time-great rosters comes up. As far as position players went, Tom Tresh spent most of the season at shortstop because Kubek had been called to active duty with the National Guard, and instead of Yogi, Hector Lopez got most of the playing time in left field. Yogi was 37 then, which was very old for an everyday player, and his career had begun to wind down; Ralph Houk, my old Denver manager who'd replaced Casey as Yankees skipper in 1961, put Yogi in a utility role, playing mostly outfield and catcher.

He would only play one more year, retiring after the '63 season on his way to becoming the Yankee manager. But even at his advanced age, Yogi still had some gas in his tank. On June 24, against the Tigers in Detroit, he caught an entire 22-inning, seven-hour game, going three for 10 at the plate. The Yankees finally won it 9-7, with Jim Bouton, a rookie who fought Rollie Sheldon all season for the fourth-starter slot, getting the win with seven innings of three-hit ball—in relief!

Our relief corps was where another big change occurred in 1962. Luis Arroyo, who'd been so lights-out in '61, hurt his arm in the spring and was never the same pitcher. Like Yogi, he'd retire after one more season. The bulk of the save opportunities went to Marshall Bridges, who'd come over from the Reds in a swap for catcher Jessie Gonder. Bridges would have by far his best season in the majors with our '62 team, going 8-4, with 18 saves and a 3.14 ERA.

I had the best year of my career as well, and not just because of a World Series that gave me a good measure of redemption for the Mazeroski homer two years earlier. In 1962, I became an American League All-Star for the first and only time, leading the league in wins (23, against 12 losses), games started (39), innings pitched (298.2), and batters faced (1191). I even ended up as one of the top 15 vote-getters in the MVP balloting. My 23 wins were the most for a right-handed Yankee pitcher since 1928, when George Pipgras went 24-13. If you count my two wins in the Series, those 25 were the most since the original Yankee Stadium was built in '23. I'd also gotten two saves in relief.

I was kind of proud of that total, especially since Yankee Stadium, with its short right field porch, favored left-handed pitchers. They had a real advantage in that park.

Although I'd had what would turn out to be my best season ever, over-all the team was down a little. Mickey and Roger hit 30 and 33 home runs, respectively, and while those are very decent power numbers, they weren't the 54 and 61 of a year earlier. The team as a whole hit 41 fewer homers than it had the season before, losing 13 more games and finishing 96-66.

Still, we were good enough to win the pennant, ahead of the second-place Minnesota Twins by five games—a team I'd gone 5-0 against during the regular season, which I like to think made the difference in the standings. Our World Series opponents would be the San Francisco Giants, a team hungry for a world championship. The Giants hadn't won a

World Series, or even a National League pennant, since 1954, when Willie Mays had made his famous over-the-shoulder catch of Vic Wertz's fly ball in game one of the Series. They'd been the New York Giants then, moving to San Francisco four years later, and their West Coast fans were eager for the Giants' first World Series as a California-based team.

The series started on Thursday, October 4, at San Francisco's Candlestick Park, and we split the first two games. Whitey won the first one 6-2, pitching a complete game, and I was the loser in the second, throwing seven innings of five-hit ball but ending up on the wrong end of a 2-0 score. Half of the Giants' runs against me came on a Willie McCovey homer leading off the seventh inning.

Just after I lost that game, our second son, Gabe, came into the world. He was born in Tanya's hometown of Larned, Kansas, where we lived in the off-season.

Back at Yankee Stadium on Sunday, we won the third game 3-2 and lost the fourth 7-3, with my old teammate Don Larsen, now a Giant after bouncing around a little, winning it in relief. That was on October 8. Set for the next day in New York, the fifth game was rained out, so we didn't get to play it until Oct. 10, a Wednesday. I started and managed to throw a complete game; we won 5-3.

So we were up one when we moved back to Candlestick for the conclusion of the series. But because of more bad weather, this time on the opposite side of the country, we had to wait around for five days before finally getting to game six. The Giants took that one 5-2, setting us up for the finale.

If there hadn't been any rain delays, Jim Bouton—who'd had a pretty good rookie season with us—would have been in line to start the seventh game. Instead, because of the long layoff, I got the start, even after having pitched all nine innings of game five. The same thing went for the Giants' ace Jack Sanford, who'd gone 24-7 that year, leading his team in wins, and finishing second (behind the Dodgers' Don Drysdale) in the Major League Cy Young Award voting. He and I would be going head-to-head for the third time in the Series, with one victory apiece, so it was our personal rubber game. And once again, I was going to be on the mound for a Game Seven, which would mean that the World Series was likely to be won or lost on my shoulders.

The night before the final game, after the defeat in San Francisco that knotted things up at 3-3, several of us Yankees had gathered around a hotel room bed to play a little poker. Too many years have gone by for me to remember all of the half-dozen or so Yankees there, but I know that the group included Yogi, Elston Howard, Hector Lopez, Clete Boyer, and me. We were playing seven-card stud, and the stakes had gotten pretty high. All of the cards Yogi had showing were the same suit, with a king his best up card, so I figured it was pretty obvious he had a king-high flush. He kept raising and raising until he and I were the only

two left. I had a heart flush going, so I stayed in, called him, and got my last card—the ace of hearts.

Boy, was he pissed off when I raked in the pot. There was about $350 in it, and 350 bucks was a lot of money then. I rolled it up, put it in my pocket, and said, "I'm leaving, boys."

Ralph in the locker room after a great night on the field.

You're not supposed to leave like that, just after you've won such a big pot, and they all tried to get me to stay.

"Nope," I told them. "When you can beat Yogi, that's a good sign." And I went back to my own room and slept like a baby.

＊　＊　＊　＊

The next day, I was interviewed by a really good newspaper writer from around the L.A. area whose name I can't recall. He brought up Mazeroski's homer, which was only natural, since I was going to be taking the mound in another seventh game. He asked about the pressure I must be feeling.

"Look," I told him, "I'm just thankful for the opportunity to pitch in a seventh game again. Win or lose, I'm ready for a second chance."

I've heard there's a word in Chinese that means both crisis and opportunity. That may be true or it may not be. I suppose I could've looked at that seventh game as a crisis, since it confronted me with the threat of being the losing pitcher at the end of two World Series, but I saw it as an opportunity not only to help the team become world champions, but also to redeem myself for the first game seven.

I thought then, and I still think, I'd acquired a little bit of a bum rap for that one. It had been a hard-fought series and a very long day in Pittsburgh—as I said earlier, I warmed up five times before I finally became the fifth Yankee pitcher used in the game. Bob Turley had started and only gone one batter over an inning before Casey pulled him for Bill Stafford, who pitched the second. By the top of the third inning, when Bobby Shantz came in, we were behind 4-0. But he pitched well for several innings and by the time the game got to the bottom of the eighth, we were up 7-4. Things unraveled for Bobby then, though, and by the time I made my appearance, replacing Jim Coates with two outs in the eighth, the Pirates were back on top by a score of 9 to 7. I managed to bring that inning to a close by getting Don Hoak, their third baseman, to fly out. And by the time I walked out to the mound to face Mazeroski, starting the home half of the ninth, we were tied 9-9.

We'd all played hard, and everybody was just worn out—their pitching staff as well as ours. The only way any pitcher on either team was getting batters out was when they hit line drives to someone. It's a strange statistic that not a lot of people remember, but in that 10-9 game, no player on either team, pitchers included, struck out. The score tells you that there was an awful lot of hitting going on, but it doesn't begin to tell you the whole story.

So two years later, the day of the final game in San Francisco, we all rode out to Candlestick on the team bus, listening to a sports show on the radio. Joe Garagiola was the commentator, and someone asked him who he thought was going to win the seventh game. Well, even though Joe was famously Yogi's pal from childhood, he was a National Leaguer all the way, having been with the Cardinals and Pirates, the Cubs and even the Giants. In those days, before interleague play, the rivalry between the two leagues was huge.

So Garagiola said, "Oh, well, the Giants are going to win. Terry's already lost one seventh game. The pressure'll be too much for him and he'll choke."

Calling an athlete a choker was just about the dirtiest rap you could come up with, and I didn't like being tagged with that label at all. So when we got out to the field, I went up to the group of reporters that were hanging out around the cage and looked around until I found Joe.

"I hear you picked me to choke," I said.

He protested. "No, I didn't, Ralph."

"The hell you didn't," I told him. "I heard you on the radio when we came over on the bus."

"Well, I had to say *something*, you know," he said, which struck me as a pretty weak response.

I looked at him for a moment. "You didn't have to say *that*," I returned, and walked away.

Even today, I like telling that story. I might not like it as much if the outcome of our seventh game with the Giants had gone the other way.

* * * *

Throughout my life, I've picked up baseball memorabilia that means something to me, and one of the newer things I've gotten is a ball signed by the umpiring staff for that seventh game in San Francisco, gotten for me by my good friend Mike Wegner. It's of historical as well as personal significance to me.

I look at that ball and I see the signatures of Stan Landes, the plate umpire, a great big guy who did a marvelous job, calling an excellent game; Charlie Berry at third, an old-timer; and Al Barlick, the second base ump, who was a very famous National League umpire. Then there was Hank Soar in right field, Ken Burkhardt in left, and Jim Honochick at first.

When a World Series goes seven games, I'll tell you which way to bet: put your money on the home team. If you go back and look at the history of the Series, you'll see a far greater percentage of home victories than visitor victories in game-seven contests. A lot of it has to do with playing before your hometown fans. Having umpires from the home team's league is a factor as well. For whatever reasons, the percentages are against you when you're playing a game seven away from your home field.

There are those who say that this particular match was one of the greatest final World Series games ever played. I know that I was very aware of the stakes going in, and I'd be lying if I said that awareness didn't lead to some anxiety. It wasn't quite as bad as the feeling I'd had before my debut as a major league pitcher in Fenway, which I told you about at the very beginning of this book, but it was close.

When you're pitching in a World Series game seven, with everything on the line, you sit in the dugout between innings, and you can't really *do* anything. At least when you're on the mound, you've got an immediate threat that demands your attention. But when you're sitting there waiting to go back out and pitch, you start thinking about what it all means, how winning or losing involves so much money a man—things like that. To keep my mind clear, I'd get up, get a drink of water, rattle the bats, anything I could think of to keep my mind clear of those thoughts.

Fortunately, the innings went pretty fast. Jack Sanford was pitching a very good game against us, and so I'd go up and down and up and down and didn't have to stay in the dugout for long stretches. Still, it's the closest I've ever gotten to feeling the way I did before that first pitch against the Red Sox in 1956.

By the time that game rolled around, Tanya was back from the hospital with Gabe, who'd only been in the world for 10 days, and Raif, who was a little over a year old. She was watching the game on TV with her mother back in Larned, Kansas, and as it went on, she finally had to leave the room and go outside, taking Gabe with her. After a few minutes, her mother came out and told her she had to come in and sit down. Tanya was so worked up about the game, her mother was afraid she was going to drop Gabe.

Even for those without any personal involvement in the outcome, it was a dandy game, especially for those who love pitcher's duels. The only run came in the fifth inning, when Tony Kubek, back from the military duty that had kept him off the roster for most of the year, grounded into a run-scoring double play. (Tom Tresh, our shortstop in Kubek's absence, started the game in left field.) Moose Skowron had led off the inning with a single to left, Clete Boyer following with a single to center that sent Moose to third. I came up then and drew a walk, so the bases were loaded when Kubek hit his grounder to short, and he and I were out. Since it was a double play, he didn't get credit for knocking in the run, and because the score ended up 1-0, no one on either team had an RBI.

I retired the first 17 hitters I faced before the pitcher, Sanford, got a little dunker over second in the bottom of the sixth inning. It was the only time in the whole game that I shook Elston Howard off. He wanted me to throw Sanford a curve, and I thought, "Naw, I'll throw him a fastball." And there it went, landing on the outfield grass barely past second base.

That was one of only four hits the Giants got off me that day. In the bottom of the seventh, with two outs in the inning, Willie McCovey tripled to deep center. He died on third when I struck out Orlando Cepeda, their No. 5 hitter. Then in the ninth, Matty Alou led off the inning by bunting to the first-base side of the field for a hit, and Willie Mays—who later told a friend of mine that I was the most accurate pitcher he'd ever faced—doubled to right. In between, I'd struck out Matty's brother Felipe Alou, pinch-hitting for the pitcher, and Chuck Hiller, their second baseman, but Matty might have scored if Maris hadn't fielded the ball so cleanly in the outfield and zinged a throw to Bobby Richardson, his cut-off man. Roger may be remembered best for his home-run hitting, but I'm here to tell you he was a great defensive player as well.

Then, with runners on second and third and two outs in the bottom of the ninth, up came McCovey, who'd gotten that triple off me in his last at bat. And the setup was in place for a classic confrontation.

NEW YO

1962 WOR

Front Row, Left to Right: WHITEY FORD, BILL SKOWRON, ROGER MARIS, TOM TRESH, JI
BOBBY RICHARDSON, YOGI BERRA.

Second Row, Left to Right: JOE SOARES (TRAINER), BUD DALEY, DALE LONG, TONY KUBEI
BRUCE HENRY (TRAVELING SECRETARY).

Back Row, Left to Right: LUIS ARROYO, HECTOR LOPEZ, JACK REED, BOB TURLEY, JC
(BATTING PRACTICE PITCHER).

Seated on Ground in Front, Before FRED

YANKEES
CHAMPIONS

AN, FRANK CROSETTI, RALPH HOUK, JOHN SAIN, WALLY MOSES, CLETE BOYER, MICKEY MANTLE,

BOUTON, ELSTON HOWARD, BILL STAFFORD, TEX CLEVENGER, PHIL LINZ, DON SEGER (TRAINER),

ANCHARD, MARSHALL BRIDGES, ROLLIE SHELDON, RALPH TERRY, JIM COATES, SPUD MURRAY

Mantle at batting practice

Houk came out to the mound, and the infielders gathered around. Since first base was open, Ralph asked me if I wanted to pitch to McCovey or load the bases and face Cepeda.

I said, "Wait a minute. Isn't that how the Giants got *into* this World Series?"

The Dodgers and Giants had ended the regular 1962 season with identical records, leading to a three-game playoff for the National League championship, which had taken place only a few days earlier. Splitting the first two with Los Angeles, the Giants had won the rubber game after Dodgers' reliever Ed Roebuck walked McCovey in the top

Tuesday, October 16, 1962 at Candlestick Park

NEW YORK YANKEES	ab	r	h	rbi
Kubek ss	4	0	1	0
Richardson 2b	2	0	0	0
Tresh lf	4	0	1	0
Mantle cf	3	0	1	0
Maris rf	4	0	0	0
Howard c	4	0	0	0
Skowron 1b	4	1	1	0
Boyer 3b	4	0	2	0
Terry p	3	0	1	0
Totals	32	1	7	0

SAN FRAN GIANTS	ab	r	h	rbi
Alou F. rf	4	0	0	0
Hiller 2b	4	0	0	0
Mays cf	4	0	1	0
McCovey lf	4	0	1	0
Cepeda 1b	3	0	0	0
Haller c	3	0	0	0
Davenport 3b	3	0	0	0
Pagan ss	2	0	0	0
Bailey ph	1	0	0	0
Bowman ss	0	0	0	0
Sanford p	2	0	1	0
O'Dell p	0	0	0	0
Alou M. ph	1	0	1	0
Totals	31	0	4	0

NEW YORK YANKEES	IP	H	R	ER	BB	SO
Terry W (2-1)	9.0	4	0	0	0	4
Totals	9.0	4	0	0	0	4

SAN FRANCISCO GIANTS	IP	H	R	ER	BB	SO
Sanford L (1-2)	7.0	7	1	1	4	3
O'Dell	2.0	0	0	0	0	1
Totals	9.0	7	1	1	4	4

of the ninth inning. At the time, Los Angeles was ahead, 4-2, but that free pass opened the floodgates, and San Francisco ended up scoring four runs and winning 6-4.

"This is a National League ballpark with a National League umpire behind the plate," I said. "Anything close, I'm not going to get the call." If I walked McCovey to load the bases and then fell behind Cepeda, I'd have to come in on him and not work the corners. Because of that, he might get something he could get his bat on, and he'd just put in an All-Star season, batting over .300 with 35 home runs.

"Let me try McCovey," I said. "I've got good stuff today. Let me try him high and tight, and if I fall behind in the count, I'll put him on."

Even though the stakes were awfully high, it was kind of a humorous meeting. Houk looked at me and said, "Well, I don't know what the hell *I'm* doing out here." And Kubek told Richardson, "I hope he doesn't hit it to *you*. You've already made one error in the Series." Willie Mays was standing there on second, listening to us and laughing.

Then it was down to business. McCovey liked the ball out away from him. He had long arms, and he could reach out there and get it. I knew he was a lowball hitter, so I worked him high and inside, just as I said I'd do.

He was a great hitter, and he did a good job of hitting the second pitch I threw him—

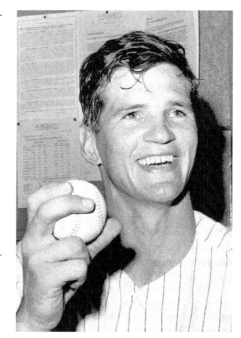

Nothing like getting the last out in a ballgame.

an inside fastball. (Mazeroski had hit the second pitch I'd thrown *him*, too.) Later, I saw film of McCovey getting on that ball, and he's leaning back, trying to get his arms extended. But he couldn't, so he hit it mostly with his hands. It was still a hard-driven ball. Luckily, we had Bobby playing in the hole, in an infield shift, and the ball sailed past me and toward him, high but catchable. Sure enough, he grabbed it, and just like that we were World Series champions, on the winning side of a 1-0 game.

The great old third baseman George Kell, working with Garagiola on the NBC radio broadcast, called it very succinctly: "Ralph Terry gets set. Here's the pitch to Willie. There's a liner straight to Richardson! The ballgame is over and the World Series is over!"

Like my old roommate Bob Turley used to say, there is no feeling like getting the last out in a ballgame. And in *this* ballgame? Well, more than 50 years later, I *still* don't have the words for it.

In all nine innings, I'd only gone to a three-ball count with one hitter, and that was their third baseman, Jimmy Davenport, in the third. I had him struck out on a two-two fastball, belt-high on the outside corner, but Stan Landes called it a ball. I came back and got him to hit it off the end of the bat to second base, a pop-up. So adding this one to my other two postseason games, I came out of the 1962 World Series with a 1.80 ERA, 25 innings pitched, 16 strikeouts against only two walks, and a 2-1 record. It was good enough to make me the Series MVP, an honor that was being awarded for only the seventh time in baseball history. And not only that. When I got the last out of that game, I became the first and so far the only pitcher in MLB history to have thrown the final pitch in two World Series game sevens.

And let me tell you, I would much rather have had it turn out the way it did than for it to have gone the other way. It was far better to lose the first one and win the second. As the old saying goes, you're only as good as your last performance.

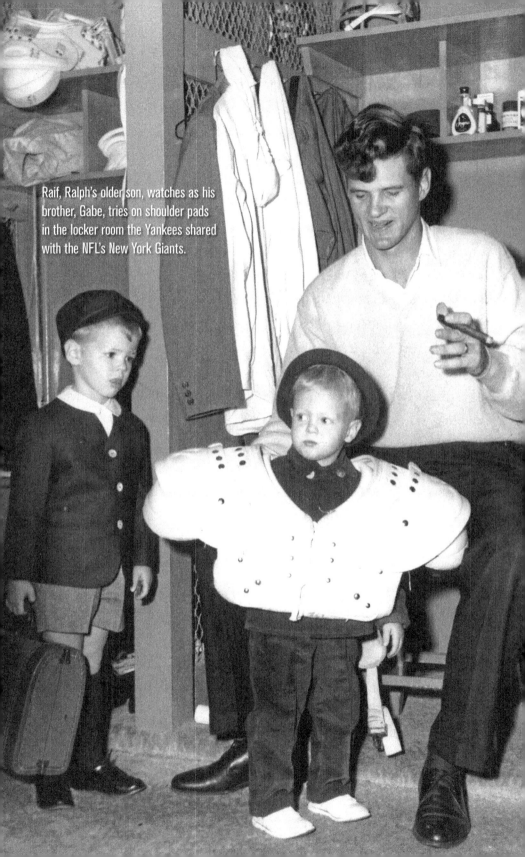

Raif, Ralph's older son, watches as his brother, Gabe, tries on shoulder pads in the locker room the Yankees shared with the NFL's New York Giants.

11

ONLY THING CONSTANT
IS CHANGE

It wasn't until after that game that I realized what a psychological load I'd been carrying around, maybe even for a couple of years, ever since the end of the 1960 series. I began to understand that I'd been dealing with just about as much pressure as an athlete can be subjected to, because I'd been handed the ball when everything boiled down to one final game. How you perform in a situation like that doesn't just affect *you*. It affects your family, your relatives, your friends, your teammates, your hometown—even your home *state*—and every single fan of your team. The Yankees have always had a terrific fan base, and those fans were great. They never held that 1960 Game Seven against me. And what's really good about that, you know, is that they all, from family to fans, had to take a lot of guff about how I was a loser. But they shared the losing *and* the winning, the sadness *and* the elation, with me. I appreciate that. They stuck with me.

I remember when I first came up, we were on the team bus outside Yankee Stadium, and fans were crowded around, wanting autographs. Mickey signed a few, and then he got tired of it and wouldn't sign any more. Phil Rizzuto, who'd been a Yankee since 1941 and was that year winding up his Hall of Fame career, sat there and signed everything that anybody stuck

THE TERRY FAMILY Ralph, Tanya, Raif, and Gabe

in front of him. I saw the look on those people's faces as they walked away with his autograph, how much they enjoyed the whole experience, and I thought, "I want to be like Rizzuto. I'll never be that big, but I want to be like Rizzuto."

He already knew what I found out later. If there's a mutual respect between a player and fans, if you remember to be kind to the people who follow you and your team, they'll stick with you through the tough spots. It's something I've never forgotten.

I forged a lot of friendships with fans, and one of them was a young man from Boston named Dan Rea. He was probably 12 years old when I

Well-known talk radio host Dan Rea with Ralph and Tanya.
Oklahoma Sports Hall of Fame Induction, 2015.

met him through a mutual acquaintance named Herb Redding, who used to travel down from Maine to watch the team during spring training. I knew the Rea family's connection to Herb, so when Dan sent me a fan letter, I wrote back, a correspondence started, and we became friends. After that, whenever we came to play the Red Sox at Fenway Park, I'd get Dan tickets for the game and take him down to meet the guys in the dugout. He was always very appreciative. A real fan.

The friendship we started back then has continued through the decades. Dan's become a well-known broadcaster, currently hosting *NightSide with Dan Rea*, a talk show on Boston radio station WBZ. Since he's a conservative in a pretty liberal city, I've told him he ought to call his program *Behind Enemy Lines*. But he has a nice way about him, talking to Democrats as well as Republicans, conservatives and liberals, and he has some very good conversations with people throughout the political spectrum. He's won several awards, appeared in the 1990 movie *Reversal of Fortune,* and when I was inducted into the Oklahoma Sports Hall of Fame in August of 2015, I was honored to have him come down and introduce me. He's a very special man, a real fan who became a real friend.

* * * *

I honestly don't know how I would've felt if I had lost that last Series game for the Yankees. Luckily for me, I didn't have to find out. Now I was able to enjoy my status as the winner of game seven. I'd gone from goat to hero, and it felt great. I remember Joe DiMaggio, that legendary Yankee from San Francisco, coming into the locker room after the game and telling me it was the greatest-pitched World Series seventh-game victory that he had ever seen.

"Del Webb is so happy," he said, referring the big-time real estate developer who co-owned the Yankees with Dan Topping. "You ought to

Two of the game's greatest hitters, Joe DiMaggio and Ted Williams, in a lighter moment.

sign your contract as soon as you can. Right now he'll give you anything you want."

General manager George Weiss had left the team in 1960, the same year as Casey, and in 1962 had assumed the same position with the newly formed New York Mets, with Casey as manager. The man who took Weiss's place in the Yankee organization was Roy Hamey, who wasn't a bad guy, but by the time we started working on my new contract, it was clear he wasn't there to give me anything I wanted.

In those days, contract negotiations were one-on-one meetings between you and the team's general manager. You could not come in with an agent, attorney, or any other representative. If you tried, they'd kick you both right out the door. It was in the grand old tradition of the game, one-on-one, except that it was like putting a goldfish in with a shark. You were dealing with financial experts, and maybe you had a little one at home, another one on the way, a house payment and a car payment and a bank loan of a thousand or two. Plus, if you were a Yankee, living in New York wasn't cheap, and you couldn't deduct your home away from home on your income taxes. Because of all this, you'd sign the first thing they stuck in front of you.

It was the same with scouts. They'd sign some good players, and when one of them made the big leagues, they'd brag about how little money it took to get him signed.

The best signing story I ever heard was about Herb Score, the brilliant Indians pitcher on the bad end of the Gil McDougald line drive I wrote about earlier. He'd been a hot prospect living in Lake Worth, Florida, and when he was old enough to sign a major league contract, his dad called all the interested scouts in and said, "All right. I'm going to work him out, and I want you all here with your best bid and no baloney." So the day came, and with all the scouts assembled, Herb started warming up.

"Okay," his dad said. "We'll start the bidding. Give me a fastball, Herb."

Whoom!

And a guys says, "Ten thousand!"

"C'mon, Herb. Put a little extra on it," said his dad.

Whoom!

"Twenty thousand!" bid one of the scouts.

"Thirty thousand!" said another.

"Now," Dad said, "show 'em your curveball." And he really snapped one off.

"Forty thousand!"

His dad auctioned him off, right on the spot, and Score ended up with a Cleveland Indians contract that included a $60,000 signing bonus. What a great way to do it.

There in Hamey's office, though, I had to negotiate the old-fashioned way. So we talked and made offers and counter-offers, and I finally got a new contract worth $10,000 out of him.

"We've never given any pitcher more than $10,000," he told me, and stuck to his guns.

That did represent a salary increase, although not a huge one, and we needed the money, so I signed. At about the same time, my Series opponent, Jack Sanford, was re-upping with the Giants for $15,000. I'd see him occasionally, and he'd always buy me a drink because he got a bigger raise than I did.

* * * *

As the saying goes, the only thing that's consistent in this life is change, and the 1963 Yankees were a changed ballclub. One of the biggest differences was at first base, where second-year player Joe Pepitone had taken over for Moose. At age 32, Moose had spent his entire nine-year career in New York, but after the '62 Series he'd gotten traded to the Los Angeles Dodgers for Stan Williams, a member of the Dodgers' pitching staff since breaking into the bigs in '58. He'd go on to do a good job as our fifth starter in '63.

Not only was Moose gone, but injuries would keep our two most famous position players off the field for most of the season. Only two years earlier, Mickey Mantle and Roger Maris, the M&M Boys, had grabbed the attention of the world with their quest to break Babe Ruth's home run record. In '63, Mickey only appeared in 65 regular-season games, hitting just 15 homers, while Roger's totals were 90 and 23. Roger fought back problems all year, missing most of the second half, while Mickey was sidelined with a foot he broke in June, tangling it in a chain-link fence in an attempt to bring down a Brooks Robinson fly ball at Baltimore's Memorial Stadium. For the rest of the year, center and right field were patrolled by a platoon of Yankees, notably Hector Lopez, who'd been starting for us in left, and Tom Tresh, with backup catcher Johnny Blanchard and light-hitting but good-fielding Jack Reed also getting some innings in as outfielders.

Although we got good production that year out of Pepitone (27 homers) and Tresh (25), no one could replace the home run power of the M&M boys. The big guy for us in '63 ended up being one of those quiet Yankee leaders I admired, Elston Howard, who hit .287 with 28 homers and 85 RBIs on his way to becoming the first-ever African-American MVP of the American League.

We began the season on the road, and I was the opening day pitcher, throwing a six-hitter against the A's in Kansas City's Municipal Stadium, the park where I'd met Tanya back when I was on the Kansas City roster. We won it 8-2. At the close of the season, my numbers may not have been as spectacular as the year before, but I think they were pretty solid: along with a 17-15 won-lost record and a 3.22 ERA, I led the American League in games started (37) and complete games (18), and finished just behind the Indians' Dick Donovan in walks per nine innings, 1.223 to 1.310. I don't remember the WHIP stat being around at the time, but I later found out that I topped the league there, too, allowing a combined average of 1.063 walks plus hits per inning. Those last two stats make me think again about what Willie Mays said about my accuracy, which was one of the best compliments I ever received.

My old roommate Whitey Ford beat me in total innings pitched by only one and a third, something that would figure in when I negotiated my contract for the '64 season.

In spite of the injuries and changes, the '63 Yankees actually won eight more regular-season games than the '62 team, finishing the year at 104-57. But we also had the misfortune of becoming the first Yankee club to be swept 4-0 in the World Series. We had another good pitching staff that year; both Whitey and Jim Bouton won over 20 games, and Al Downing, who'd stuck in the rotation for the first time, won 13 with almost a strikeout an inning. But the Los Angeles Dodgers starters, led by Sandy Koufax in his prime, quieted our bats, and we went down in four games—losing two to Koufax, one to Don Drysdale, and one to Johnny Podres. We did have Roger and Mickey back in a limited capacity, but Roger went 0 for 5 and Mickey hit .133 with a single homer in 15 at-bats. (On the other side, Moose went 5 for 13 with three RBIs against us, while the guy he was traded for, Stan Williams, pitched three innings of one-hit ball in game one.)

I pitched three innings in the second game, taking over in the top of the sixth for Downing and allowing one run on a Willie Davis double to right followed by a Tommy Davis triple to center. (Unlike the Alou boys I'd faced in the Series the year before, Tommy and Willie were only teammates, not brothers.) All in all, a much quieter World Series for me, which wasn't necessarily a good thing.

* * * *

After getting to the big leagues, Ralph Houk, I believe, became a better manager. But after three years, he moved up to the general manager position, and the just-retired Yogi Berra took over as the field manager for our 1964 season.

As I mentioned earlier, Ralph Houk and I had our differences, both when I played for him at Denver and later on in New York. Now he was my general manager, the guy I had to negotiate with for my '64 contract. And if you thought we didn't see eye-to-eye there, too, you'd be right. As I wrote earlier, I'd won 17 games and led the league in a couple of categories in '63, and I believe I would've led in innings pitched, too, if—as the Yankees' manager—he hadn't sat me down for the last week of the season. I ended up with 268 innings pitched, and Whitey got 269 1/3. Pretty close, but I came in second.

So we argued and argued, and finally I got a $500 raise out of him. Later on, I saw him in spring training, and he told me, "I'm surprised you signed for that."

I don't mean to suggest that Ralph Houk was a bad guy. He had his reasons for doing what he did. But he and I just saw things differently. Finally, I told him, "As long as I get the ball every fourth day, we'll be fine. I won't worry about the rest of it. Just let me have the ball and roll me out there."

As it turned out, that didn't work out quite as well as it had the past few seasons. I began to be pestered by arm problems, and I didn't get any work until our twelfth game of the year, against the Washington Senators in the second game of a doubleheader at Yankee Stadium. I started, pitched six innings, gave up three runs, and took the loss. That was kind of a portent of things to come. With Yogi using me as both starter and reliever— I started 14 games and finished nine, out of a total of 27 appearances—

I ended up 7-11 with a 4.54 ERA, my first losing season since '59, and my first ERA above 4.00 since '58.

It was a strange year for the Yankees. Although we ended up 99-63 for the season and played in our fifth straight Series, we always seemed to have our backs to the wall. This time, getting into the World Series became a continuous uphill battle. We rallied to have a great September, and we needed it. It was only in the final week that we passed the White Sox, ending up one game ahead in the standings and winning the American League pennant.

We went all seven in that Series with the St. Louis Cardinals. I closed out Game Four at Yankee Stadium, coming in to start the eighth with the score 4-3 in their favor. That was the final score as well. I pitched the eighth and ninth, gave up two hits, struck out three, and didn't walk anyone. But since that was the only time I pitched, I wasn't too much of a factor. Neither was Roger Maris, who'd come back from his injuries to once again be our starting right fielder. He'd had a good regular season for us, but he just hit one homer, for his only Series RBI, in those seven games, ending with a World Series batting average of .200.

Mickey was back, too, and he followed a terrific '64 season with a very good performance in the Series, going 8 for 24 with three homers and eight RBIs. I remember being in the dugout with him during the second game, which was played at Busch Stadium. It was the ninth inning of a contest we'd end up winning 8-3, and by this time the game was getting away from the Cardinals. Johnny Keane, the Cards' manager (who'd become the Yankee skipper in '65), brought in a left-hander named Gordon Richardson, who had a pretty good curveball. He threw one to Mickey, and Mickey knocked a bullet over third that hit the chalk and went for a double, scoring Roger from first. A couple of batters later, Mickey scored on a Joe Pepitone single to right, and he came in and sat down beside me.

"Mick, how's that left-hander?" I asked. "Has he got pretty good stuff?"

"You know that double I got down the left field line?"

"Yeah."

"I wish it would've gone foul," he said. He meant it, too.

Bob Gibson, at the beginning of his long run as a dominant National League starter, had good breaking stuff and a little three-quarter tailing fastball that he threw over the top, kind of like a sinker. He started that second game, going eight innings before throwing complete fifth and seventh games on his way to being named World Series MVP. He struck out 31 Yankees in the Series, but he allowed 11 runs, too.

In the final game, Mickey was responsible for three of them. Ahead 6-0 in the sixth, Gibson made the decision to just throw smoke and challenge Mickey to hit his fastball. In his two previous at-bats, Mickey had struck out and grounded back to the pitcher, so it's easy to understand Gibson's confidence.

He got the first one by Mickey, and then he came back with more smoke and Mickey, batting left-handed, got hold of one. One of the famous Busch Stadium features was a huge Anheuser-Busch logo, high atop the left field fence, with an animated eagle that flapped its wings whenever the home team hit a home run. Mickey's homer nearly hit that eagle. I mean, he really tagged it. That son of a bitch went halfway up the bleachers.

The next time Mickey came up, in the eighth, Gibson pitched here, pitched there, nibbled around, really worked on him, and got him to fly out to center. He gave up a couple more homers in the ninth, to Clete Boyer and Phil Linz, but Gibson and the rest of the Cardinals held on to win the game and the series, 7-5.

* * * *

I guess the most famous, or infamous, story about the 1964 Yankees has to do with utility man Phil Linz—the guy who'd fooled around with self-hypnosis—and his harmonica playing in the back of the team bus after we'd lost four in a row to the White Sox at Comiskey Park in late August. (I took the loss in the first one, a 2-1 game.) Linz was in the back playing "Mary Had A Little Lamb," and Yogi, sitting in front, hollered for him to knock it off. Allegedly, Linz didn't hear what Yogi said and asked Mickey, "What did he say?"

Mickey, joker that he was, said Yogi had told him to play louder. Linz did, and this led to the famous altercation, with Yogi slapping the harmonica out of Linz's hand. Somehow, that incident said a lot about the nature of the team that season.

A lot of baseball historians have written that 1964 marked the final year of the so-called Yankee Dynasty, which stretched clear back to 1920, when Yankees owners Jake Ruppert & Col. T.L. Huston bought a converted pitcher named Babe Ruth from the Boston Red Sox. If it really was the end of an era, it coincided with the end of my career as a New York Yankee. That came ten days after I'd made my only appearance in the '64 World Series. It would be the last time I'd wear the Yankee pinstripes.

Back in early September, the Yankees had made a deal with Cleveland for the veteran starter Pedro Ramos, intending to make a reliever out of him. To get Ramos, they'd sent $75,000 to the Indians, with the agreement that Cleveland would get two players to be named later. Bud Daley was one of those players.

I was the other.

12

A TOUCH OF CLASS IS IMPORTANT

Gabe Paul was the general manager of the Cleveland Indians, and I went in during the off-season to talk to him about my salary. I'd made $38,000, I believe, the year before with the Yankees, and that's what I asked him for. He countered with an offer of $30,000.

"Wait a minute," I told him. "You picked me as the player you wanted to complete the deal for Ramos, so you must've thought I could do a good job for you."

He said that was true, and we went back and forth for a while. Finally, he suggested that I sign a contract for a base of $30,000. *But* for every game I won over 10, I'd get another $1,500, on up to 15 games. So the upshot was that if I won 15 games, I'd be just about back to the $38,000 mark. To sweeten the deal, he told me I'd also get performance bonuses for every win after that. So, he told me, I'd essentially be signing a contract for $38,000 with a chance to make even more.

I knew that the pitcher with the most wins for the 1964 Indians was Jack Kralick with 12, so I figured it might be tough to get 15 with this team. And I knew I'd had an off-year in '64. Still, I was confident I could bounce back, so decided to go ahead and roll the dice with him.

Ralph pitches for the
1965 Cleveland Indians

I also knew what he was offering me was illegal at the time under major league baseball rules. It was a performance contract, which ties a player's salary to certain levels of achievement. Those are standard now, but in 1965 you couldn't make that kind of a deal. There were no bonus clauses in major league contracts.

Still, when I sat down with him to talk money, that's what he offered me, and that's what I took. He drew up the agreement, I signed it, and he put it in his safe. I never got a copy, which is my fault.

The first half of the season went very well for me. In fact, I think I should've been an All-Star that year. At the break, I was 9-3 as a member of the Indians' rotation with Luis Tiant, Sonny Siebert, Jack Kralick, and my roommate Sam McDowell. One of my nine wins had come on May 5, when the Yankees visited Cleveland Stadium and I'd been matched up against Whitey. It was the first time I'd faced my old team since being traded, and all I allowed that day was a Bobby Richardson single in the first inning, a Tom Tresh bunt single in the second, and, in the sixth, an infield hit to Pedro Gonzales, who was pinch-hitting for Whitey. I even hit a double off my former teammate. We won 4-0—a complete-game, three-hit shutout—and I did it with 70 pitches. Although pitch-count wasn't an

1965 Cleveland Indians

official statistic then, that was the lowest number of pitches in a complete game since the World War II years, and it hasn't been beaten since. (The Orioles' Jose Bautista tied it in 1988 with a 1-0 loss to the Mariners.) The game was finished in a brisk hour and 39 minutes.

But even though I knew I'd shut them down decisively, I didn't make a big deal about beating my old team. That wasn't my style. I did want to show the Yankee brass they'd made a mistake when they traded me; I figured the best way to do that was just pitch as well as I could and keep my mouth shut. What's that they say about winning being the best revenge?

The great old Yankees shortstop Frank Crosetti, who went clear back to the Babe Ruth-Lou Gehrig days, was their third-base coach at the time, and the next day he came over during batting practice and said, "Ralph, I'm really proud of you. You showed a lot of class. We've traded guys and when they beat us, they blast us in the newspapers and everything. You beat us, but you never popped off about it."

I thought that was a nice gesture on Frank's part. "Thanks," I told him, and then I said something about how the team wasn't the same as it had been a couple of years ago. I'm sure he agreed.

While the fans have always picked the position players for the All-Star Game, the managers of the teams that played in the previous year's World Series usually name the pitchers. I say "usually" because every once in a while there are exceptions.

Nineteen sixty-five was one of those unusual years. If things had been normal, Yogi, as the 1964 Yankee manager, would've picked the American League pitchers and 1964 Cardinals manager Johnny Keane would've done the same for the National League. Both, of course, would've then managed the teams from their respective leagues in the All-Star Game. But in an odd series of events, Keane had replaced Yogi as the new Yankee manager, while Yogi had gone to the National League as a coach of the

New York Mets. (He technically ended his career as a player there, after not playing at all in '64. With the '65 Mets, he got into four games, mostly as a pinch-hitter, going 2 for 9.)

Because of all this moving around, the baseball brass decided that the managers of the runner-up teams in each league would be the All-Star Game managers for '65. That meant it was the White Sox's Al Lopez and the Phillies' Gene Mauch choosing the pitchers. (The Phillies and Cincinnati Reds had actually tied for second in the National League, but Reds manager Fred Hutchinson had died of lung cancer in November '64.)

As I said, I was 9-3 at the break with a good ERA, and maybe if Yogi had been managing the American League All-Stars, I would've been chosen. But he wasn't, and Lopez didn't pick me.

After the break, I won another game and then, all of a sudden, I wasn't being used any more. So I went in to see Birdie Tebbetts, the manager.

"What's happening?" I asked him. "You're not pitching me."

"Well, Ralph, we've got these young pitchers, Tiant and McDowell, and some other guys, and we're wanting to see what they can do," he told me. "We've fallen behind Minnesota in the pennant race, and we'll make a run at it next year."

"That's fine, but I've got a contract with Gabe, and he assured me he'd give me the opportunity to pitch."

"I run this ballclub," he said. "That's between you and Gabe. I don't know anything about it."

Of course, he knew *all* about it. He and Gabe had worked together for years in Cincinnati before coming to Cleveland.

So day after day, I sat on the bench. In late August, when we went to Dodger Stadium to play a four-game series against the Los Angeles Angels, Tebbetts finally gave me a start. It was the fourth game, and I pitched pretty good, throwing seven innings of five-hit ball. We won 8-2, and that made my record 11-4. I had one more appearance on that road trip, a no-decision start against Kansas City we ended up winning, and that was it.

When we got back to Cleveland in early September, I went in to see Gabe Paul.

"Are you satisfied with the job I'm doing?" I asked him.

"Oh, yeah. You're doing a great job."

"You sure you didn't get a lemon, or a pig in a poke?"

"Naw," he said. "Not at all."

"Well, then," I returned, "here's the problem. Birdie says he's not going to use me. He's going to the younger pitchers to see if they can make the staff. Why don't we just throw my contract out, and if I'm doing a good job for you, just give me the salary I made last year with the Yankees."

"Don't worry about a thing," he said, patting me on the back. "I'll take care of you. Come see me when the season's over."

I barely pitched for the rest of the year. Tebbetts put me in to relieve a couple of times, but most of the time I didn't even get near the bullpen. We could be losing by six runs, and I *still* wouldn't get the call to warm up. They were afraid I'd luck out and get a win.

As the season was winding down, Jack Kralick got hurt, so I got a couple of starts, but I was out of shape and lost them both—one to Mel Stottlemyre in New York and the other to Mickey Lolich in Detroit. So I ended the year at 11-6, with a 3.69 ERA. All things considered, I thought those numbers were pretty good, so I went in to see Gabe Paul again.

He looked up from his desk like he was surprised to see me. "What are *you* doing here?" he asked.

"Well, the season's over, and I came to see you, like you said."

"Well, you won 11 games, so you get $31,600 for the year."

I felt myself starting to get mad. "Well, that's a hell of a deal," I told him. "You ask for me in a trade, I have a good year for you, and you cut my salary almost 25 percent?"

"I've been in baseball 40 years. A deal's a deal."

"That's no way to treat someone," I said. "That's not right. You just lost a ballplayer. I'll never pitch another pitch for you."

"Oh, *you'll* be back," he said. "You can't make this kind of money on the outside."

Now, I *was* mad. "That's a *terrible* argument to use with a ballplayer," I said. "How about this? The hell with you, and the hell with Cleveland."

At that moment, I was mentally divorced from baseball. I loved the game, but I hated the general managers. So I walked out, passing Charlie Morris, the club secretary. He was a good, hardworking guy. If you ever needed tickets to a game for anybody, he'd take care of it. He always looked after us, and, to show our gratitude, my teammate Rocky Colavito and I had bought him a nice watch that year and had it engraved: "To Charlie from Rocky and Ralph." He said it was the nicest thing anyone had ever given him.

Now Charlie was outside the door, laughing his ass off about what I'd just told his general manager. The last two things I heard were Charlie Morris laughing and Gabe Paul hollering, "*You'll* be back!"

I'm sure he thought I would be. But I held out and didn't sign a new contract, and on April 6, just before the season started, he traded me to the Kansas City A's for John O'Donoghue, a left-handed pitcher, and cash.

* * * *

Although this story probably belongs later on in the book, which deals with my post-baseball golf career, I feel like I should tell it now. Years after my blowup with Paul, I was down in Tampa, Florida, playing on the Senior PGA tour. One day, late in the afternoon, the clubhouse guy came in and said, "Ralph, there's a man here who'd like to see you. He says his name is Gabe Paul."

My first thought was that someone was trying to kid me. I had friends who knew that Paul was the man who had soured me on baseball. And there were some practical jokers in my circle.

"Sure," said, "send him in."

I'm not sure if I really expected Gabe Paul himself to come through the door, but he did, along with some big shot from Anheuser-Busch, which had a big plant down in Tampa. Paul seemed kind of apologetic when we shook hands, and I figured it would be best to let bygones be bygones. There was no real reason to stay mad at him—sure, he'd screwed me in a contract deal, but I was doing fine in my life after baseball and besides, I've heard it said that holding a grudge is like taking poison and hoping the other guy dies.

So I introduced him and his friend around to the other golfers, and we went to the clubhouse, had a drink, and buried the hatchet. In fact, after a little while we were actually able to laugh about what had been so serious then. He figured it might still be serious, too. At one point, he told me he wasn't at all sure if I was going to let him in when he knocked on the clubhouse door.

* * * *

'll end this chapter with another story involving golf and the Cleveland Indians. One July day, playing on the road in Southern California, we had an off-day or a night game—I can't remember which—and Bob Neal, the Indians' announcer, and I went out to play golf at the Bel-Air Country Club in Los Angeles. Eddie Merrins, the pro at the course there, said, "Let me get you a couple of guys to play with." There were two men looking at clubs on the rack in the pro shop, and Eddie brought them over. I've forgotten one of their names, but I won't ever forget the other.

"Shake hands with so-and-so and Jim Stewart," Eddie told us.

He had a beard, but when I saw those blue eyes I knew him immediately.

"Jimmy Stewart," I said. I was shaking hands with one of the biggest movie stars who ever lived.

At the time, he was working on *The Flight of the Phoenix,* but production had shut down for a week because the famous stunt pilot Paul Mantz had died when the plane used in the movie crash-landed. That day, Stewart's companion was a high-ranking Air Force officer, and they both talked about flying a lot. Jimmy Stewart himself was in the Air Force Reserve.

We teed up and played, and Stewart was tickled to be with a good golfer. "I'm a hacker with a 25 or 26 handicap," he told me, "so I never get to play with good players."

When we went to lunch, I asked him about making *The Stratton Story*, the movie that starred him as Monty Stratton, the old White Sox pitcher who shot himself in the leg. He had to have it amputated, but he was fitted with an artificial leg and actually came back and pitched in the minor leagues for several more years, although he never made it back to the majors. Stewart told me they bent his leg behind him and strapped it up, and then put on an artificial leg. He was a slender guy, of course, and the uniforms were baggy, so no one could tell his leg was doubled up behind him.

He gave me his phone number and I told him, "You come to New York, and we'll play." That didn't happen, but I really enjoyed the day and learning about what he went through to play one of my fellow major league pitchers—especially one who had to work through as much adversity as Monty Stratton did.

13

THE ULTIMATE PROMOTER

In 1966, the old Yankees pitcher Eddie Lopat was GM of the A's. But the deals were made by Charlie Finley, the team's colorful and controversial owner. He was the one who'd offered O'Donoghue and cash for me.

I knew that meant Finley figured I still had something left, and he'd probably give me a chance to prove it. Still, I wasn't sure I wanted to take the deal. Still stung by the way Gabe Paul had treated me, I was mentally prepared to leave baseball for good. I'd spent most of the spring playing golf, hustling up games, and I was up about $2,500 in side bets when I got the phone call from Finley.

I told him I'd report to the A's if he could get Major League Baseball to void that illegal contract Paul had given me and restore the rest of the $38,000 I felt I was due. I also said I'd join the A's if he'd pay me that same salary.

"Let me talk to the commissioner," Finley said. "I'll see if something can't be done about your Indians contract."

At the time, the Commissioner of Major League Baseball was a man named Spike Eckhart. I don't think he was exactly a baseball man, but he was a retired Air Force Lieutenant General, and maybe the owners thought he'd be a good contact man for Washington, with the Vietnam War heating up and players going in and out of the service. That's just a guess; I don't know. Anyhow, Finley called me back a few days later and said, "I went to a meeting and presented your case to a four-man council, and I didn't get to first base."

He told me that Walter O'Malley, the Dodgers owner, was one of the members, along with Pirates owner John Galbreath. Time has erased my memory of the fourth person he mentioned, but the third was someone I knew very well: Gabe Paul. His presence on the board sure didn't help my cause any.

The upshot was that I wouldn't be able to get the salary that I'd worked myself up to before signing that deal with Paul.

Charlie Finley was considered a maverick by the other owners, who kind of resented him, so he was probably doomed to fail in his efforts to get my salary restored. At least he went to bat for me, though, and I appreciated that. Plus, I liked Finley. He was a very interesting guy. I remember that he wanted me to sell insurance for him in the off-season, and he gave me this advice: "When you go out with a client, you talk two things: baseball and insurance. Baseball and insurance. Those are the only two reasons they're out with you. They don't want to hear about politics or world affairs—it's baseball and insurance. Stick right to that, and you'll make a million." I always remembered that.

When it came to salary, Finley told me he couldn't give me the $38,000 I wanted, but he'd give me a little more than the base salary I'd gotten from Gabe Paul. And he was persuasive. He told me it'd be like coming home, since I used to play for Kansas City. He also knew I was living in Kansas in the off-season, in Tanya's home town of Larned. It was less than 300 miles from KC, so I'd be close to my family for much of the season.

He finally convinced me to play for the A's, and while that team would finish in seventh place that year—ahead of the Senators, the Red Sox, and the dead-last Yankees—some of the pieces were already in place that would lead to the three consecutive World Series championships in the early '70s, following the team's move to Oakland in '68. They had Bert Campaneris at short, Phil Roof catching, and a real good second base-man in Dick Green. Blue Moon Odom was starting to pitch regularly. Sal Bando was on his way up. Catfish Hunter had made the team a year earlier, at the age of 19, and 20-year-old Rick Monday would get called up from the minors that year.

After I signed, Charlie sent me down to Daytona Beach, Florida, where I spent a couple of weeks getting into shape. I got into my first game with the A's on April 30, the twelfth game of the season, when manager Alvin Dark used me for two innings of relief at Yankee Stadium—one hit, no runs. After relieving in another game a few days later, I got my first start at home on May 10 against Boston, pitching five innings and allow-ing one run on three hits, getting a no-decision in the 3-2 win.

I didn't win my first game until June 22, but it was a sweet victory, coming against the Cleveland Indians at Municipal Stadium. I pitched six and a third innings, allowing one run, and we beat Gabe Paul's team 11-4.

A few days later we were playing the Baltimore Orioles, and I was in the game as a reliever. When Frank Robinson came up, I jammed him with a pitch in on the fists, and he hit a little dribbler down the third-base line. I was wearing new spikes at the time, and when I came off the mound and planted my foot to throw him out, the spikes snagged on the grass and I buckled. I managed to get off the field, but my ankle immediately swelled up. It turned out to be a sprain, and it was bad enough to put me on the disabled list for several weeks. I didn't do much when I came back, ending my stint with the A's after 15 games—10 as a starter and five as a reliever—with a 1-5 record but a pretty good ERA of 3.80. On August 6, Charlie sold me to the New York Mets, where I went 0-1, with one start, one save in 10 relief appearances, and a 4.74 ERA to end the season. I also finished six games, one of which is worth noting because it was the only game in which I'd ever face Hank Aaron, who'd lead the league in homers (44) and RBIs (127) that year.

I'd known Hank for years. A lot of people don't know that when he first came up with the Milwaukee Braves in '54, he hit cross-handed, one hand over the other. Of course, they changed him right away, but I don't imagine anyone thought a skinny kid who batted cross-handed would ever be the one who'd break Babe Ruth's record for home runs in a career.

When I was with the Yankees, we'd play the Braves a few times in spring training. They were one of several teams that were training around Tampa, Florida, at that time. We'd come over from Fort Lauderdale and stay in a hotel, and a lot of the other teams would, too. One day, Bobby Richardson and his wife were coming out of our hotel when some guy—I don't know if he was drunk or what—came up to Bobby and got really belligerent, pushing him and trying to start a fight. Just about that time, along came Hank Aaron, who was there with the Braves. .

Bobby, at 5' 9" and about 170, wasn't the biggest guy in the world, but six-foot-tall Hank was a pretty imposing figure. That didn't stop the man who'd accosted Bobby. He took a couple of swings at Hank, and Hank gave him a short right to the midsection. It only took one. I'd always thought it was great of him to step up and help little Bobby.

I pitched to Aaron twice on August 27, 11 days after Charlie Finley sold me to the Mets, working the last three innings of a game we lost 3-0 and allowing three hits and no runs. I also got two strikeouts, both in the sixth. The first man up in the inning was Hank, and he kept fouling me off. It got to be 3-2, and I was throwing some real good pitches on the outside corner. Finally, I let loose with a fastball, but it was about cap-bill high, and he chased it and struck out.

Aaron was unusual in that he hit down into the ball and it came off his bat with backspin. Most of your big home-run hitters have an uppercut swing and hit the ball into the air, but Hank hit it a different way and got that backspin.

I faced him for the second and last time in the eighth and got him to hit a flyball to center. So one of the greatest hitters ever to play the game ended up 0 for 2 with one strikeout against me. That's a pretty tiny sample size, but I'm still proud of it.

* * * *

My solo start for the Mets that year came on August 11, five days after I'd signed, at Forbes Field in Pittsburgh. The Pirates still had Bill Mazeroski at second—he played in every one of their games that season—and they were a good team, with an outfield of Willie Stargell, Roberto Clemente, and Matty Alou.

It was the first time I'd faced Maz since that seventh World Series game, and I had an idea. I got with him before the game and said, "How about this? The first time you come up, I'm going to throw the first pitch way over your head, high up on the screen, like I'm pissed off."

He thought that'd be funny, so that's what I did. Even though it was almost six years later, most of the crowd knew exactly what was going on. I think they appreciated it.

After that, I got down to business and retired him on a fly to center. He got an RBI single off me in the third, but the only time I faced him again, in the fifth, he popped up to Ed Kranepool at first.

Going into the sixth inning, we were up 5-2. I got into a little trouble then, giving up a double to Clemente followed by singles by Jose Pagan and Donn Clendenon around a Stargell groundout, so Westrum brought in a left-hander, Rob Gardner. When I left, I was up 5-3 with two runners on. Pinch-hitter Andre Rogers promptly hit a single off Gardner, scoring another run credited to me. Still, at the end of the sixth we were up 5-4.

Gardner did a pretty good job until the ninth inning, when Matty Alou led off with a single and Maz bunted him to second. Then Clemente singled and Gardner hung a curve to Stargell, who deposited it in the stands. There went my victory. We lost 7-5.

I remember an inning in that series when we had our leadoff hitter, Al Luplow, on third with one out. Before becoming a professional baseball player, he'd been a halfback at Michigan State, and he was fast, so when one of our guys hit a long fly to right he tagged up and took off for home. Clemente was on the warning track in right field and he caught that ball and threw in on a line to the inside corner of the plate, knee-high. It never bounced. Bang-bang—it's right there. It hit the catcher's mitt and Luplow slid but was out. That's still the greatest throw I ever saw.

The only other time I faced the Pirates that season was a few days later, at Shea Stadium on August 18, when I finished a game with three innings of one-hit ball, striking out the side (including Maz) in the eighth. It was my only save, and my final one as a major leaguer. Come to think of it, that earlier game in Pittsburgh would mark my final major league start. Sure, it's coincidence, but I find it kind of interesting that both my last save and last start in the big leagues were against Bill Mazeroski's team.

14

FRIENDLY ADVICE

As usually happens with any ballclub formed by an expansion draft, the New York Mets weren't a very good team for their first few years. In fact, the 1966 version was the first *not* to lose 100 games in a season, finishing 66-95. The Mets had first taken the field in 1962, with soon-to-be 72-year-old Casey Stengel as manager. Thanks in great part to Casey and his charisma and quotability, the Mets had quickly established a fan base in spite of, or maybe *because* of, their losing ways.

By the time I got to the team, Casey was gone, having been replaced by the old New York Giants catcher Wes Westrum toward the end of the '65 season. (Westrum had been a member of the Giants when Willie Mays made that legendary catch of Vic Wertz's fly ball in the 1954 Series.) He had a young team in '66. Another National League team, the Chicago Cubs, had started having some success with a youth program, bringing up young players and giving them starts over veterans, so the Mets had begun the season with that plan as well.

Sometimes a youth program works, and sometimes it doesn't. If you shove a lot of kids in there before they're ready, they get bombed and can lose their confidence, which hurts a team in the long run. But the strategy had clicked for Chicago, so the Mets brass figured it was worth a try. The reason I was put on the roster later in the year, along with other veteran pitchers like Bob Friend and Bob Shaw, was just to help finish things out.

At the end of the regular season, the team sent me to the Florida Instructional League, which ran for a couple of months in September and October. I had been working on developing a knuckleball, figuring that maybe I could extend my career as a relief pitcher. The Mets saw some potential there, too, so they wanted me to work on the knuckler for a few weeks in Florida.

While I was down there, I started hanging around a little with a 22-year-old left-hander who had just finished his second season with the Mets, jumping right to the big club from Single-A in 1965. Tug McGraw wasn't exactly setting the National League on fire, going 2-7 in '65 and 2-9 in '66, but he was the only Mets starter who'd beaten the Dodgers' Sandy Koufax, and that was a big reason they kept him around. He had a big curve ball and a pretty good fastball, which he threw with a beautiful overhand delivery. Later on, he'd nickname his fastball Peggy Lee, after the famous singer who had a 1969 hit called "Is That All There Is?"

We got to be friends, and on an off-day in Florida, we went out to play golf. Of course, we talked baseball while we were going around the course.

"Right-handers are giving me a lot of trouble," McGraw admitted. "I've got this big curve, and the umpires don't like to call it. If it comes over knee-high, the catcher catches it around the batter's ankles, and it doesn't look like a strike, so the umpires look bad if they call it. If the catcher grabs it in the strike zone, the umps say it's too high. I get ball one, ball two, and then I've got to come in with a fastball. Pretty soon, one of those big right-handers catches hold of it, and I'm beat. What do you think I should do?"

I said, "Well, I'll tell you what. You need another pitch, and I can show you how to throw a screwball. It'll give you a different off-speed pitch with a little movement, and it won't put any strain on your elbow.

"About ten o'clock, we'll go out to the ballpark, and I'll get Jerry Grote or one of our other catchers to come out then, too. We don't need any coaches around. And I'll show you how to throw that pitch."

So we went out the next day, and I showed him how to put the grip on the ball, to twist with his fingers and throw it overhand. You do that right, and the fingers kick back and really put a sizzle into the ball. When you come overhand, batters look for the ball to drop and level off, but with a screwball it goes sideways, and you've got *deception.*

So I showed him the grip and the way to throw it and had him try it. It was like teaching a duck how to swim. I'm not kidding. In no more than 10 or 15 minutes, he had it. I never dreamed that he'd pick it up so quickly. But he did, and it was beautiful.

"That's it," I told him. "You've got it. Straight over the top. You look like Warren Spahn. Now use it. It'll get 'em out."

With the youth movement in full swing, the Mets released me on November 30 so that they could bring someone up to fill my roster spot for the next season. But I was invited to spring training, and McGraw was there, throwing the pitch I'd taught him. He was looking *good,* too. Opposing batters were eating out of his hand.

His newfound success soon attracted the attention of the Mets' bullpen coach, Sheriff Robinson, a former catcher and baseball lifer who'd kicked around in the minors for a dozen years before getting into coaching and managing. One spring day when Tug came in off the mound, Robinson said, "What's that pitch you're throwing?"

"Oh," he said, "that's a screwball." He looked over at me. "Ralph showed me how to throw it."

Oh, shit, I thought. I didn't want to be a pitching coach, and I sure didn't want to look like I was trying to take Robinson's job. But that's the way he looked at it. I was his potential rival. Even before that, while I was having a real good spring, I knew Robinson was turning in bad reports on me, telling management, "Get rid of Terry, and keep so-and-so."

Robinson looked me up and down and then turned back to McGraw.

"You're too young to be throwing that, kid," he said. "Don't do it any more."

So now Tug McGraw was under strict orders not to use the screwball. And he started getting bombed. At the beginning of the '67 season, he went 0-3 in four starts with a 7.79 ERA, which resulted in his demotion to the Jacksonville Suns in the Triple-A International League. And still, the Mets didn't want him throwing a screwball.

He spent all of '68 with Jacksonville, and at some point he decided the hell with it and made the decision to throw the screwball after all. Baseball fans know what happened after that. As the top reliever for the 1969 Amazin' Mets, he shot to stardom. In the early '70s, he was so big that he was able to get a national syndicate to pick up a baseball comic strip called *Scroogie* he'd created with artist Mike Witte. By that time, everyone knew about the screwball, or scroogie, I'd taught him back in '66.

Sheriff Robinson, meanwhile, was gone at the end of the '67 season, although he scouted for the Mets until nearly the end of the '70s.

I beat him out of the Mets dugout by a few months, though.

* * * *

In 1967, the Mets were starting to build a decent team. Jerry Grote, their catcher, had been up for a couple of years, and in May, they got Ed Charles from the A's to be their starting third baseman. He was another veteran and a really good defensive player. For a while, he was just about the only guy in that infield you could count on to pick up a ground ball and make a play. Tommy Davis was in left field for his only year as a Met; he'd end up leading the team in homers (16), RBIs (73) and batting average (.302).

Ralph with his son Gabe

The youth movement was still on, and in addition to McGraw, who didn't stick, two other future pitching stars came up to the parent club that year: Jerry Koosman and Tom Seaver. Like McGraw, Koosman wasn't quite ready, but Seaver was. In his rookie year, he went 16-13 with a 2.76 ERA—the ace of the staff.

In spring training that year, down in Lakeland, Florida, Westrum started him against the Tigers. They had Al Kaline, Norm Cash, some good fastball hitters. So Seaver went out there and got bombed in the first inning. He was throwing nothing but fastballs, and I mean it was a swing and a miss, a swing and a miss, and then—boom!—a double off the wall. Swing and a miss, swing and a miss, strikeout. Next guy, swing and a miss, and—boom!—a home run. They teed off on him.

Finally, he got the third out. Bob Shaw and I, two old-timers, were sitting in the dugout watching him and wondering out loud how the youngster was going to take it. He came in, threw his glove down, and said, "Screw it. They hit everything I threw at 'em. I need a beer."

I thought, "Well, this kid's going to be all right. He's going to make it."

Another time Seaver and I were talking about a player who hit 18 home runs in a season but had 30 more that were caught right up against the fence. He called it warning-track power.

"You know," he said, "if I hit 30 or 35 balls a year that were caught on the warning track, I'd go crazy. I'd do anything I could, pushups, whatever it took, to get that extra 10 feet when I hit a ball."

That's the way he thought. From the very beginning, he was a terrific competitor, and I wasn't at all surprised when he developed into a superstar.

* * * *

The '67 Mets had just as many veterans on their roster as kids, and I was one of the former. I had a real good spring as a non-roster invitee, so just before the season started, they signed me as a free agent. Over the next couple of weeks, I pitched two outings of relief, giving up only one hit, no runs, and striking out five in 3.1 innings. On what would turn out to be my last game, on April 22, I closed out a 4-3 loss to the Phillies at Shea, pitching two innings, allowing no hits, and striking out three, including their star third baseman Richie (then Dick) Allen, who was beginning the third of his three consecutive All-Star years. I didn't know it then, but he would be the last major league batter I'd ever strike out.

Following those two appearances, I was set up to make a start against the Cincinnati Reds, but it got rained out. Then general manager Bing Devine called me in.

"Well, Ralph," he said, "I'm going to have to give you your pink slip. We're releasing you."

I didn't say anything.

"Sit down," he told me. "Let's talk about it."

I looked at him. "Ain't nothing to talk about," I said. "You just gave me my release from baseball. This has been my life. I'm 31 years old, and I know what I can do. I'm in good shape. I had a good spring. I'm throwing the ball well. And I'm telling you right now that you've made a mistake. I may never, ever get a chance to prove you wrong, but if you want me to sit here and tell you that you did the right thing, you're not going to hear it. You made a mistake."

I believe it was mostly a salary thing. Right around that time, they began releasing a lot of their best-paid players. In addition to me, before the '68 season they also got rid of Ken Boyer, who'd been the National League MVP in '64; Tommy Davis, who still had a lot of good years left as a player, especially after becoming a designated hitter in the American League; and three good pitchers, Bob Shaw, Fat Jack Fisher, and me. We were their top five salaried players. They finished dead last that year and still drew more than a million and a half people to Shea Stadium. After us, their highest salaried player was their first baseman, Ed Kranepool, making $23,000. So financially, the team was a big success.

The day Devine called me in and released me, we were living in a rented house up in White Plains, New York. A friend of mine named Monk DePalo came over. His son, Jimmy DePalo, and I had both pitched in the Yankees farm system, and we'd roomed together in Denver. He was a good pitcher who never made it to the bigs.

When Monk heard the news, he was stunned.

"How can they do this?" he asked. "I don't understand."

"Monk," I said, "I've got two week's severance pay and the sun's shining. Let's go play golf."

We went to Westchester Country Club and played 36 holes. And that's how I left baseball.

15

ONE SHUTS, ANOTHER OPENS

May 16, 1967 was the day Bing Devine released me from the Mets. Technically, it was my last day as a major league pitcher. But the break wasn't completely clean, especially after George Weiss called me and apologized for my being cut from the Mets roster.

Before becoming the Mets' first general manager, Weiss had spent a long stretch—from 1948 through 1960—in the same capacity for the Yankees, so I'd played for him and knew him. When Charlie Finley sold me in August of '66, George, at the age of 72, was winding down his days as the Mets' GM. Replaced by Devine, his former special assistant, for the '67 season (the only year Devine would be general manager of the Mets), George stayed with the organization in a reduced capacity. He may have become a vice president or consultant; whatever his title, he continued to work for the team behind the scenes.

The call I got from him after being let go by the Mets really made me feel good. He said, "Ralph, I want you to know that I didn't make that decision. It was all Devine. And I can get you a tryout with the Cubs if you'd like."

"Sure, George," I told him. "That'd be fine."

He was as good as his word, and a few days later I was working out with the Cubs. They had a good team in '67, with Ron Santo, Ernie Banks, and

Billy Williams, Fergie Jenkins, Don Kessinger and Glenn Beckert—all those guys. I worked with them for a few days, but my time as a potential Cub ended one day when all the pitchers were running in the outfield and I tripped on something and twisted my knee. So I didn't really get a chance to show the team what I could do.

Not long after that, while the season was still in full swing, the Cincinnati Reds called and wanted to sign me. By this time I'd been off for a few weeks, so there was a stipulation that I had to go down to the minors and pitch until I could get back into shape. I gave the offer some pretty serious thought but finally declined.

Looking back on it, I think I was spoiled by being on those great Yankees teams—seven of them pennant winners—and sharing a locker room with guys like Mantle and Maris and Yogi. I just wasn't mentally prepared to head down to Buffalo, New York, and play for the Triple-A Buffalo Bisons, with the old lockers and the cold jock straps. After well over a decade as a major league pitcher, I wasn't hungry enough to go out and beat the bushes all over again.

So that did it. The 18-year-old raw rookie from the sandlots of Chelsea, Oklahoma, had gone on to beat the odds and not only make it to the bigs but enjoy a pretty damn good career with the greatest franchise in the history of the sport. I knew I could *still* get batters out, and I probably could've hung in a while longer, but at the age of 31, I didn't want to keep pitching badly enough to go back to the minors and prove myself all over again with kids barely out of their teens.

I've been asked a lot if I ever thought about returning to pro ball as a coach. Thinking back on it, I might've enjoyed coaching for Ted Williams, whom I knew pretty well. Whitey Herzog would've been a good man to work for, too, and I had a chance to do that. Back in the late 1980s, Whitey asked me to coach for him at St. Louis.

"What I want you to do," he told me, "is get 'em in shape."

By this time, I'd been a pro golfer on the Senior PGA Tour for a couple of years and was doing pretty well. "Whitey," I said, "I'm a golfer, and I'd want to play golf whenever we went out on the road." The Cardinals played in Chicago, L.A., all these big cities with great courses, and when you've got night games, you can golf during the day.

"Sure. That'd be fine. We play golf."

"I don't mean with the coaching staff. I need to work on my own game. And when the season's over, I don't want to go to some winter league or instructional league. I'd see you when spring training started, and that'd be it."

"No, no, Ralph," he said. "We can't do it that way. We work all year long." I was pretty sure that would be his position; he had a reputation as a workaholic. And while I knew he was a smart man and would've been a good guy to coach for, I wanted to play golf and hunt pheasant and ducks in the wintertime. So it didn't happen.

* * * *

In 1963, my next-to-last year with the Yankees, several partners and I had started looking into buying a golf course. Our head man was Jerry Volpe, a great golfer who taught me a lot about the game. He was a big Yankee fan, and he always made us players welcome at the club where he worked as a pro, Englewood Golf Club in Englewood, New Jersey, just across the George Washington Bridge. It's long gone—Interstate 80 runs through it now—but in the early '60s it was a big deal. Most of the clubs then were all Jewish, or all Italian, or all WASP. They didn't mix much. But Englewood was an open club with mixed membership. It was close to Manhattan, too, so a lot of entertainers would come across the bridge and tee up. I played golf there with Buddy Hackett, Joey Bishop, and Phil Foster, who's best remembered now for playing Frank DeFazio, Laverne's dad on the old *Laverne & Shirley* sitcom. I hit balls with Ed Sullivan. Jerry gave lessons to

Ralph with fellow golfers and star Los Angeles Dodgers pitcher Sandy Koufax.

the trailblazing black athletes Jackie Robinson and Althea Gibson, who was the first African-American woman to compete in international tennis competitions. Later on she became a professional golfer. I played a lot of golf with her in the '60s, when the private courses still weren't open to blacks. Whenever she or Jackie came to Englewood, though, they were always welcomed.

Englewood's celebrity connections didn't end with the golfers who visited the course. When I was playing there in the '60s, Jim Lee Howell, who'd coached the New York Giants football team from 1954 through 1960, lived on the club's 13th hole.

With Jerry Volpe in our group to help and advise us, we went looking for a course to invest in. It didn't take much time before we'd found a little one up for sale for $200,000 or $300,000, and we were ready to buy it, but the guy took our bid and used it to jack up someone else who was interested. So we dropped out.

Eventually, Jerry's father-in-law saw an advertisement in the *New York Times* for a 205-acre estate in Morris County, New Jersey, located in an upscale area of the state near Morristown. The neighborhood was known as Far Hills, and it was home to some unbelievable mansions. Diamond Jim Brady's old estate was there. The Roeblings, whose patriarch, John, built the Brooklyn Bridge, lived nearby, as did Aristotle Onassis. After we bought the estate and built the course, Jackie Kennedy Onassis used to ride by, hunting foxes back in the hills with the Essex Hunt Club. They'd come through shouting, "Tally-ho! The fox!" Their hunt usually took them by our fourteenth hole, a par five, and sometimes she'd be out there with the hunt master and the dogs, and she'd stop and watch the golfers and wave.

Buildings on the property included a 41-room, red-brick English Tudor mansion and a set of fireproof stables constructed with Belgian bricks. It had been owned by an old railroad baron named Walter Phelps Bliss, who'd died in the '20s. He had three daughters, and one of them, Priscilla Mallory, lived on a little farm right on the edge of the property. She was the last one standing, and she wanted to sell.

When we first went up to see the estate for ourselves we immediately knew it was something that would suit our needs. But before we could transform it into a golf course, we had to come up with an agreement that would satisfy the representatives of the two townships the property was on, Mendham and Bernardsville.

It's funny how golf and baseball have intersected so often in my life. Our attorney in these proceedings was a man named Bernard Shanley, who'd been White House Counsel for President Eisenhower in the early '50s and was at the time with Shanley & Fisher, the biggest law firm in Newark, NJ. He was also an old baseball man. He'd played third base for Columbia University when Lou Gehrig was pitching and playing first base for the team. He'd been in Yankee Stadium on July 4, 1939, when Gehrig had delivered his "luckiest man on the face of the earth" speech.

With Bernard in our corner for the township negotiations, we argued that the golf course would actually preserve the land around the estate, and, after much discussion and lots of meetings, we were finally granted a variance on their zoning laws that allowed us to have a golf course on the property. So we bought the place for $240,000 and started in, converting the stables to cart and equipment sheds and that huge mansion into our clubhouse. We hired Hal Purdy, an architect who specialized in golf course design, and a construction man, and at one point we had twenty laborers on the grounds, picking up stones around the hilly areas that would become our course.

All of that started sometime in 1964. It took somewhere in the neighborhood of two years to complete the conversion process, and once it was ready, we christened it the Roxiticus Golf Club; as I remember it, "roxiticus" is the Delaware Indian word for "meeting place." The club opened just as my major league career was winding down.

Although I didn't know it then, the timing couldn't have been better. For years, I'd been playing during the off-season on a great course called Prairie Dunes in Hutchinson, Kansas, about an hour and a half east of my house. A young golfer named Pat Thompson was assistant pro there. He'd grown up in Mission, Texas, where my brother and father lived, and gone on to win a championship for Texas University. I knew him and liked him, so I offered him the same position at Roxiticus, working with Jerry Volpe, who had become our general manager as well as head pro.

Pat took me up on the offer, but after being there for a while, he realized he just didn't like the East very much. Also, his girlfriend lived back in Hutchinson. So, homesick and missing her, he returned to Kansas. His departure took place just after Bing Devine cut me loose from the Mets.

Pat's return to the heartland meant that Roxiticus was suddenly in need of a club pro to work with Jerry and the members. And I was an athlete and a serious golfer who had just lost his job as a major league pitcher.

So in June of 1967, only a few weeks after Bing Devine had given me my pink slip, I decided to get into professional golf and went to work as a club pro at Roxiticus, teeing 'em up, renting carts, selling golf balls.

At that time, if you wanted to be a professional golfer, you just declared yourself one and then applied to the PGA, the Professional Golfers Association. You went in like an apprentice for four years, and you had to go to classes and pass a final test. As I remember, the exam had five categories—equipment, greenskeeping, management, inventory, and teaching. It was a very difficult test. I was told after it was graded that I was the only guy in the history of the New Jersey section of the PGA to make a perfect score. A lot of it was multiple choice, so luck had something to do with that.

I was also lucky to have Jerry Volpe at the club to teach me the ropes. And now that I think of it, another piece of luck for me was getting to be around one of golf's all-time greats just as I was making the transition from professional pitcher to professional golfer. It was Jack Nicklaus, and his welcoming me into the ranks of pro golfers is something I've never forgotten.

Ralph with his Palm Springs Baseball Classic trophy.

That happened the same month I started as a pro at Roxiticus. In June 1967, the 67th U.S. Open was being held at the Baltusrol Golf Club in Springfield, New Jersey, just down the road from our course. Jack Nicklaus not only won the tournament that year, he also set a new scoring record, needing only 275 strokes for 72 holes, one shot better than the former record holder, Ben Hogan.

I knew Nicklaus. He had a place in Fort Lauderdale, Florida, and in 1962, when the Yankees moved to Fort Lauderdale from St. Petersburg, I met him for the first time at Coral Ridge Country Club. Robert Trent Jones, the famous golf course architect, was an owner of the club, and Lew Worsham, who was head professional at Oakmont in Pittsburgh, was the wintertime pro at Coral Ridge. After playing an exhibition match there with Worsham and Julius Boros, Jack was made an honorary member of the club, which gave them three U.S. Open winners: Worsham, Boros, and Nicklaus, who'd won his first Open that same year.

Jack also had some baseball ties, having played high school and American Legion baseball as a catcher in his hometown of Columbus, Ohio, backing up Johnny Edwards, who later on had a good major league career with the Reds, Cardinals, and Astros.

On Saturday, June 17, 1967—a little over five years after Jack and I had become acquainted—I was down at the Open at Baltusrol, watching the competition and talking to the participants. Jack had asked me to stick around for a while, so after he finished his third round, I was sitting on his golf bag, watching him hit balls on the practice range, his caddy shagging for him. He was a power hitter then; when he hit a ball, the ground shook.

I watched him for a while, and then I asked, "What are you working on?"

"Well," he told me, "right now I'm working on a fade. You see that telephone pole down on the left-hand side of the driving range? That's my line. I don't want anything going left of that. If it fades three feet or 30 yards, it's still on the fairway—a fade goes out high, drops, and sits down.

But if you hit a hook, it goes out there and runs and goes a long way, until a lot of times it runs into the rough or into trouble.

"You can't win the Open out of the rough," he added. "Look how high that rough is out there."

I had another question for him.

"Have you ever worked with a hook in your career?" I asked. (For those not familiar with golf terms, a fade—for a right-handed golfer—describes a shot that goes left and curves back to the right, while a hook is just the opposite.)

He nodded. "In my younger days, when I was 18 or 20, I worked with a hook off and on for about two years. It gave me nothing but headaches."

After watching him drive the ball, I understood why he'd abandoned it. He had so much power he didn't *need* a hook.

We talked for a little while longer, and then he gave me what I see now as a kind of blessing—or, at least, a welcome to the world of professional golfing. "Ralph," he said, "I hate to see you leave baseball, but you'll really enjoy golf. That golf bag is going to take you to a lot of places."

Jack Nicklaus was right on the money. It has.

* * * *

Making the commitment to be a club pro at Roxiticus meant that my family and I had to live in New Jersey during the golf season. During the winter, though, I came back home to Kansas, and since I wasn't working at the club then, I was free to play in tournaments. As a new pro, one of the first places I traveled to play was South Africa. A group of us got together, some of the Roxiticus Club members chipped in to help me with expenses, and we flew over and spent about six weeks, playing against some very tough competition, really getting a taste of what it meant to be a pro. You didn't have to qualify. You just went over there and teed it up.

There were some great South African golfers around then, people like Gary Player and Harold Henning. Plus, all the British players, the great Ryder Cup winners, went down there in the off-season. It was their Florida. We flew into Johannesburg and played there, then Capetown and Port Elizabeth and up to the capital, Pretoria. I played in Durban, down on the Indian Ocean. And on top of seeing a lot of new country and some great courses, I made a few bucks.

I enjoyed the trip so much that first year that I went back the next, this time with Tanya, who really made the most of her time there. While I was playing, she went out on tours and experienced the cultural side of the country.

The first time, the flight went from New York to Rio de Janeiro. We were traveling coach, and all the way down we were packed in like sardines. At one point, the strap under my seat broke and I sank down so far that I might as well have been riding on a toilet seat. When we got to Rio, we had an eight-hour layover before our flight to Johannesburg. During that time, we were able to go out and see a famous jewelry store, Stern's, and they showed us diamonds that were just unbelievable. When we got back to the airport, a stewardess from our Brazilian airline, Varig, came into the waiting room and said, "I've had three cancellations in first class to Johannesburg—I'll take you and you and you."

As one of the fortunate three, I spent the second leg of our flight in a very comfortable first-class seat, enjoying champagne and lobster prior to our landing at our destination.

My time as a golf pro at Roxiticus lasted until 1974. Because we'd been a little bit undercapitalized going in, we gave the membership a lease on the club with an option to buy. When the members decided they wanted to exercise that option, we had to agree on a mutual appraiser. The one we decided on came back with what our side saw as a ridiculously low appraisal, especially considering the upscale area we were in. We contested the appraisal he'd turned in and eventually found out that he had done business in the past with someone on the membership side, which made his numbers look a little shady. Finally, we all ended up before a judge in Morristown, who said, "All right, boys. Here are some yellow pads. There's an empty room back there. Go in there and get this thing settled. If you don't, I'll settle it *for* you."

It took a lot of work and plenty of compromise, but we reached an agreement. I guess our side did all right; as the original investors, we got back about three times the money we'd put in. But the settlement ended my years as a Roxiticus club pro.

When I returned to my home in Larned, I was actively competing in PGA events, but it was mostly little things: some mini-tours, several state opens, things like that. Then, out of nowhere, another opportunity to extend my golf career came my way.

One day I was talking to the president of the local golf club, Hillis Bell, and he told me that they had an old course out on a hill that had once been a sand-green course. (That's a course whose putting greens are sand instead of grass.) A few years earlier, the golf coach from Oklahoma State University, Labron Harris Sr., had come out and redesigned it, replacing the sand greens with grass and doing a real nice job.

"We haven't had a pro out here for 30 years," Bell told me. "Now we need one. So I've got a question for you, Ralph. Would you consider being our pro?"

I didn't have to think about it long. "Okay," I said. "I've got to have a club contract to retain my Class-A PGA status. But there's nothing in the rules about how much I have to make as a club pro. So I'll stock the golf shop with the necessities, balls and gloves and tees and shirts and caps and such, and I'll run your tournaments, your championships, all of that. In turn, you can give me a salary of a dollar a year."

Needless to say, he went for that in a heartbeat.

"One more thing," I told him. "I want to start a junior clinic there."

"Members only?"

"Nope. Any kid in town."

"What age?"

I said, "I'll take 'em when they're four years old if they've got the attention span to stay in line and not clobber one another. And if they don't have clubs, we'll cut off some clubs for them to use."

The membership agreed with my proposal, and the first year, we had a grand total of eight kids show up—with two dropping out.

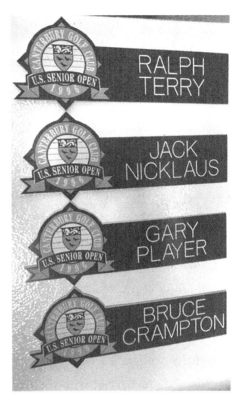

Locker tags for Golfing with Legends event, 1996 Canterbury Senior Open.

Gary Player (black hat), Ralph Terry, and Roberto De Vicenzo (right).

The next year, though, we had 12. Then 18, 24, 48, 54, 72, all kids from our small town. We put 45 of them through college on golf scholarships. One of our boys won the Missouri Valley Conference championship, and another placed 10th in Big 12 competition. A guy from Hutchinson, Kansas, named Bruce Vaughan won the Senior British Open not too long ago, and he came right out of our little golf course. He didn't start playing until he was 19 or 20, but we had lots of kids who began much earlier. Our high school girls won eight or nine state championships, our boys three.

That whole experience showed me what amazing things kids can do if they have the right motivation and training. When a club starts a junior clinic, a lot of times the head pro will send his assistant out to work with the kids instead of going himself, but I think that's a mistake. Young boys and girls who are just beginning to learn golf really need the best instructors they can get, so they'll at least be fundamentally correct with their grip, their alignment, and their swing. After that, you can let 'em develop. But if they start out wrong, they'll end up down the line on a dead-end street and have to back up and start over.

Teaching golf, really, is just correcting errors, and there are only a handful of those. You spot 'em, correct 'em, and that's it. Even though there have been a lot of big, thick books written on the subject of golf instruction, it all boils down to getting rid of a few mistakes.

One time, I was out in Midland, Texas, I think it was, for a tournament that Gary Player won. He was at the top of his game then, and a couple of other golfers and I got into a conversation with him. One of us asked him exactly what it took to be a champion, and in response he pulled out a little slip of paper and a pen.

"Well," he said, "swing is one part of it." And he wrote down *swing mechanics.*

"You always have to putt, so that's pretty important, too." So he added *putting* to his list.

He continued. "You're usually going to have two or three rough holes, when you get into a little bit of trouble, so you've got to be able to get out of that." Down onto the paper went *perform under adversity.*

As we watched and listened, he kept talking, pausing only to write three more things down.

"You've got to keep your mind on what you're doing," he told us. "When you're leaving the green, going to the next tee, look straight ahead. It's not, 'Hi, Billy. Hi, Mary. How's the family?'

Stay focused, he wrote.

"When you miss a green or go into a sand trap, and you've got to recover and make that little chip shot or whatever, you have to remember that if you let up for a minute someone could beat you by one stroke. Nicklaus was the best at that. If I made one little mistake, he had me."

Be persistent.

Finally, he had this to tell us: "For a non-contact sport, golf is very punishing. When you're playing for fun and have a bad hole, a double- or triple-bogey, it's okay. But when you're playing in a tournament, it hits you like a ton of bricks.

"This game is going to disappoint you," he added. "Some of the worst things are going to happen just as you've started going well. It's very frustrating. You have to love punishment."

And he wrote down, with a grin, *love punishment.*

I took that piece of paper with those six little things written on it, and I always remember to pass that wisdom on to kids when they tell me they want to be tournament golfers. In a few words, one of the sport's greatest summed up everything anyone needs to know about playing the game of golf at its highest level.

16

SEE THE WORLD WITH THE PGA

The PGA is divided into 41 affiliated parts across the country, which are called sections. When I returned to Kansas, I became a member of the Midwest Section, which includes parts of both Kansas and Missouri. I ended up winning our section's championship by five shots, competing against some very good golfers.

At that time, all sectional champions were given the right to go out on the PGA Tour, so that winter I decided to try my luck and see if I could get into four or five tournaments. I got in the PGA's two best ones out West, the Bing Crosby Pro-Am in Pebble Beach, California, and the Los Angeles Open at the Riviera Country Club. There were a dozen spots open on the Crosby, only about four on the Los Angeles Open. I remember being in L.A. and looking up at the scoreboard, seeing all the big names who were competing right alongside me.

One of my playing partners at the Riviera was Paul Azinger, who was a rookie that year. Then at Pebble Beach, at the Crosby, I played with another first-year pro named Larry Mize, who would become famous for the incredible chip shot he made to win the Masters at Augusta in 1987. Paul and Larry were two of the nicest qualifying rookies—rabbits, we called 'em—I ever met. I had a chance to tell them so years later, after they'd become great champions. They were both special people.

I also qualified for the Quad Cities Open in Illinois and in Davenport, Iowa, but I didn't make the cut after two rounds in Davenport, so I didn't earn any money there. I did get a good amount of seasoning, though, some valuable pro-golfing experience, and in 1986, when I turned 50, I went down to Florida to see if I could qualify for the Senior PGA Tour that year.

There were only eight spots available on the tour, so it was very difficult to get in. After two rounds I was in second place, and then I got word that my stepfather, Charlie Dawes, had passed away. I had to pull out of the tournament and return to Chelsea for the funeral. Before I could even get back to Oklahoma, a call came with more bad news: my longtime great friend and fellow baseball player Galen Hudspeth had died as well. So I had to leave the tournament, head back to my hometown, and bury two men who'd been very important in my life. It was a tough time.

The next year, I was back in Sarasota, Florida, trying again to qualify for the Senior Tour. It got down to the last two spots, No. 7 and No. 8, and

Golf Digest
The #1 golf publication

Age Shooter

Certificate of Recognition

presented to

Ralph Terry

on July 24, 2001   at age 65 played the

Mariah Hills Golf Club   in   65   strokes

Jerry Tarde
Chairman and Editorial Director

Ralph in the late '80s in front of the leader board at the Senior British Open.

three of us were in a playoff to see who got them. I parred the third hole and my opponents both bogeyed it, so I got in.

I can't remember which golfer said, "What a difference one stroke can make in your life." Whoever it was sure knew what he was talking about. All of a sudden, I got to play the full schedule. I was being treated great, with a courtesy car and a lot of other perks. When you qualify for one of those spots, you're going to make money. There's no doubt about it.

After I got in, I ended up playing in 106 Senior Tour events. I had five Top Ten finishes, made the cut in five Senior British Opens, and finished as the 15th Low Pro over in Britain one year. That meant I had the 15th best score in the whole tournament, and that was pretty good. The best senior players in the world played the Senior British Open, and they had a couple of amateurs in there who were excellent golfers, too. I think one of the reasons I did well in England was that the conditions were similar to what I'd grown up with on the Oklahoma prairie and, later, played under in Kansas: a lot of howling winds and hard ground.

The Royal Lytham & St. Annes Golf Club was a host course for the Senior British Open, and one time as I was waiting to tee off, I was talking to the starter, telling him some of the funny stuff that Yogi Berra had said.

"Oh yes, oh yes," he told me. "We know Yogi Berra. We love Yogi Berra." He kept after me to tell him more Yogi stories, and so I got his address, and when I returned to the States I sent him some Berra material.

To me, it was just another example of the impact those Yankee teams and their players have had all over the world, and how blessed I was to be a part of them.

* * * *

On top of all the traveling, both in the US and abroad, I met and got to know the greats of the game, people like Ben Hogan, Lee Trevino, and Chi Chi Rodriguez. It was Chi Chi, in fact, who got me one of the sweetest golf-related jobs I ever had.

It was in the very late 1980s when I was contacted by a representative of the Sands Hotel and Casino. It turned out the casino owners were looking for a sports host. They already had Phil Esposito from hockey and Alexis Arguello from boxing working for them, but they wanted to hire another professional athlete to go along with a golf course they'd acquired in Atlantic City.

Chi Chi did a lot of work for the Sands, and he told them, "Ralph would be a natural for you. He plays golf on the Senior Tour, and he played baseball for the Yankees." A lot of the casino's big players came from around New York and New Jersey, so having someone from a Big Apple pro sports team was a good fit.

Tanya and I flew up to New Jersey, and I met with them on a cold January day. They offered me $80,000 a year and a two-bedroom villa on the coast. In return, I was expected to hang around the golf course 15 days a year and take care of the high rollers—give them clubs, play golf with them, whatever they wanted. While we were there, we could go to all the Sands' shows, Sinatra and Wayne Newton and Harry Belafonte, on and on. I can't tell you all the big-name acts I saw at that casino.

It was a very good deal. Once in a while, they'd say something like, "We're going to go on a dinner cruise. Would you mind getting on the boat and going with us?" But there weren't really any demands from anyone, and they were nice people.

So were my fellow sports hosts, including Arguello, the welterweight fighter who'd had some famous bouts with Aaron Pryor. One of them, an HBO-televised match from the Orange Bowl in Miami in November 1982, was later dubbed "The Fight of the Decade" by *The Ring* magazine. Alexis lost it in the fourteenth round. "I hit him with everything I had," he told me. "I finally just ran out of gas."

I gave Alexis golf lessons, and we had some fun playing together. Later on, he went back to his home country of Nicaragua and ran success-fully for political office. He supposedly committed suicide, but evidence exists that suggests he was assassinated. He was a good man and I was very sorry to hear about his death.

* * * *

In 1990 or '91, not long after Operation Desert Storm began in the Persian Gulf, one of the vice presidents called me in.

"Ralph," he said, "people are sitting on their discretionary income right now, and my job is to do the dirty work. I'm supposed to let all you sports hosts go."

"I understand," I told him.

He held up a hand. "But," he added, "I grew up going to Yankee Stadium watching you play ball. Get me two Yogi Berra autographs, and you've got the same deal next year."

It didn't take me long to get on the phone to my former catcher and good friend.

"Hey, Yog. I need two balls."

"Sure, Ralph."

That vice president gave me another year after that, and when he finally had to let me go, he felt so bad he was in tears.

"Hey, don't worry about it," I said. "I've had three great years here, and I've gotten the pink slip from a lot of general managers in my time."

I can't remember if I added, "And most of them weren't half as nice as you've been." But I'll bet it crossed my mind.

*　*　*　*

Around that same time, an amazing thing happened. Bill Mazeroski was involved, but that's not the most amazing part of it.

Let me say here that Mazeroski is a very nice guy, but he's pretty private. Sometimes I think he's trying to live *down* his fame. However, when I was on the Senior Tour in Pittsburgh, the guy who ran the tournament thought it would be a smart idea to pair him with me in a pro-am tournament that was scheduled before the regular Senior Tour tournament. So Bill and I teamed up and did well, finishing third. The most memorable thing about that day was that I had a hole-in-one.

What's even more remarkable, though, is that it wasn't the only hole-in-one I made that week—and on the same hole, to boot.

You don't have to know much about the game of golf to know how rare a hole-in-one is. According to *Golf Digest*, an amateur golfer has about a one in 12,500 chance. For a pro, the odds go down to one in 2,500. (I've racked up 25 over the years, which seems to me to be kind of amazing.) I have no idea how astronomical the odds of getting two on the same course—the same *hole*—in one week would be, but I did it. First, on a Wednesday with Maz during the pro-am. The notice went up on the scoreboard: "Ralph Terry. No. 13. Hole-in-one with a five-iron. 183 yards." And everybody's saying, "Well, you should've done that on the weekend, Saturday or Sunday, because you would've made $15,000."

"Geez," I thought. "They're really rubbing it in." I felt bad about missing out on that dough.

Then on Sunday, I was playing in the Senior Tour tournament with pros Bobby Wynn and Charlie Sifford, the first African-American to play on the PGA Tour, who was known for the big cigars he smoked. We came up to the thirteenth hole, and they'd put out some grapes and stuff. We ate a bunch of grapes, and then I teed up. The pin was over on the right this time; I could see just the top two-thirds of it. I shot right in there on the pin, with a nice bounce, and I noticed that the flag fluttered a little.

The same people who'd marshaled the hole on Wednesday were out there, and they just *exploded*. I could hear them clearly: "Good God! He did it *again*!" Charlie almost swallowed his cigar.

All he could say was, "It must've been the grapes."

So up goes the notification on the message board. "Ralph Terry. No. 13. Hole-in-one with a five-iron. 183 yards." I go into the clubhouse, all pumped up, and *no* one says "nice shot" or anything else. It took me a while to realize they just figured the announcement was still up from my Wednesday hole-in-one.

But it wasn't, and I got the $15,000 to prove it. Not only that, it got me into a special tournament down in Jacksonville later that year, restricted to guys who'd made a hole-in-one on a PGA-recognized course that year.

* * * *

Although baseball is pretty tangential to that story, a lot of the other experiences I've had in my golf career, as I wrote earlier, have been intertwined with my earlier life as a major leaguer. Sometimes the tournaments have just allowed me to once again hang around with other ballplayers of my era. I remember playing in an Alvin Dark tournament in his hometown of Lake Charles, Louisiana, with a lot of other ex-big-leaguers, including Stan Musial. In addition to the tournament, there was a goose hunt scheduled for anyone who wanted to try his luck, which Stan and I did.

We were in a blind outside Jim Bel's hunting lodge in Cameron Parish, right next to a big wildlife refuge, with a guide and his big Labrador Retriever, Butch. So the first goose flew by, way up there 65 or 70 yards, really moving fast.

"Go ahead, Stan," we said. He was the top banana in the blind, so we gave him first shot. And he got up, shooting right-handed, and—bang!—got him first shot. The goose folded up and fell, and Butch jumped out and drug that big bird back.

It was a specklebelly goose, a very good-eating bird, and Musial was so excited when that big dog brought it in to him that he just stood there, stuttering and stammering. I'd never heard him do that before. He was really going.

Finally, after he'd calmed down a little, he told us that when he was very young, growing up in Donora, Pennsylvania, he'd gone to a Catholic school. As baseball fans know, he was a left-hander, but whenever he tried to write left-handed, the sisters would whack him on the knuckles with a ruler and insist that he do it right-handed. Weeks and months of that punishment caused him to stutter. And he said that even as an adult, when he'd hit a three-run homer or something, he'd start stammering.

Ralph and St. Louis Cardinals great Stan Musial after a successful day of goose hunting.

"This is the first goose I've ever shot, and I got him with one shot, and it was a good shot," he said excitedly. It was like he was a young boy all over again.

That's something about baseball and baseball players that I love. We were lucky enough to play a kids' game and make a good living out of it, and many of us have never really quite grown up. I mean that in the best possible sense. We're still capable of being awed, still retain a sense of wonder about things.

I remember back in 1996, when the Louisville Slugger people trucked in this huge bat on the back of a semi into downtown Louisville to help mark the grand opening of the Louisville Slugger Museum & Factory. They were having a big two-day ceremony, a private event on the first day and a public one the next. I'd played in a pro-am tournament with Jack Hillerich III, the company president, and he invited me to the first day's festivities. He'd gotten together about 15 major league stars who'd used Louisville Slugger bats, an incredible group that included Musial, Ted Williams, Ralph Kiner, Lou Brock, and Ernie Banks. I believe I was the only pitcher there; everybody else was not only a position player but also either a Hall of Famer or a future Hall of Famer. George Brett was one of the attendees who fell into the latter category.

So Ted Williams and Ernie Banks and I were sitting in the hotel lobby one morning, and Ted was holding forth on hitting, as he so often did in these kinds of situations. Ernie asked him something about how to get the best impact when you swing at a ball, and Ted said, "You hit over 500 home runs and you don't know how the hell you did it?" Just clubhouse shit, you know.

"You gonna show me?" Ernie asked with a grin.

"Sure," Ted said. "Hold your arm out here. Now which way are you stronger—this way or *this* way?" He turned Ernie's arm. "Now open your hips slowly. *That's* the way you hit a baseball."

At about this time, George Brett and Lou Brock walked over. This was in July of 1996, so George had only been retired for a couple of years, and his playing days were still fresh on his mind. You could just see the awe in his eyes when Ernie said, "Hey, George, come over here and shake hands with Ted Williams."

It turned out that the two had never met. Williams stuck his hand out. "How are you, George?" he said. And then, without any fanfare, he asked, "Who's the toughest left-hander you ever had to face?"

That's the way Ted was. Always talking baseball.

"Well," Brett said, "the Big Unit, Randy Johnson, was tough on me. After I started out one year going 0 for 11 off him, they began resting me whenever he'd pitch."

"He's a good pitcher. How were you trying to hit him?"

"Oh, I had a zone where I'd try to put it, from over the second baseman's head to left-center. I always figured he'd come in on me with a fastball and I could go to the opposite field with him."

"That's *all* wrong," Williams said. "*All* wrong. First thing you do is give him four or five inches of that outside corner, because if he hits it with his slider, you ain't going to do much with it anyway. Don't even swing at it unless you've got two strikes and can maybe foul it off. Instead, go up there looking for something from that point in, because he's not going to hit that spot every time.

"I learned that from DiMaggio, how he hit against Bob Feller," Williams added. "Feller threw 100 miles an hour and had a good curve ball, but DiMaggio was very successful against him."

Ted went on, talking hitting, and as I sat there among those Hall of Famers and one who was soon to be in the Hall, I thought about how memorable this all was, the greatest hitter of one generation giving advice to a great hitter of another, brought together by their love and passion for the kids' game we were all lucky and blessed and talented enough to play for a living.

* * * *

I'd like to close out this section of baseball-related golf stories with two more, one of which seems too coincidental to be true. They both have to do with that infamous World Series game seven in 1960, when Mazeroski's shot off me won it for the Pirates.

As Jack Nicklaus predicted on that Saturday at the 1967 U.S. Open, my golf bags ended up taking me a lot of places across the globe. One of them was the southern part of mainland Portugal, where I participated one March in the Algarve Open Pro Golf Tournament. It took place there every year at a course called Penina; Sir Henry Cotton, who'd won three British Opens, was Penina's director of golf.

The course was right off the ocean, and the weather during the tournament could get pretty bad. To help the participants warm their insides against the cold and wind, Sir Henry made sure to set out plenty of strong port wine at every other hole. In fact, the great sportswriter from L.A., Jim Murray, once wrote a piece about the tournament with the headline "Any Old Port in a Storm."

Prior to the tournament, Sir Henry had a pro-am event, and he paired me with a short and stocky Englishman named W.D.P. Norton. Old W.D.P. was a wealthy guy, the owner of a couple of steel companies. Maybe he thought his money gave him special license to be mouthy and obnoxious, because he was.

We were playing one-ball, which meant that the two of us took turns playing a single ball. That style of golf was very popular in parts of Europe, including Portugal. W.D.P. and I were paired in the tournament with two

Ralph (left) and Bobby Richardson (second from right) get ready to embark on a hunting trip near the small town of Foyil, Oklahoma.

Swedes, and although there are some very skilled Swedish golfers now, in those days most of them weren't very good. As we went along, W.D.P. kept poking at 'em, giving them hell about how their country hadn't joined the Allies in World War II, how they'd even kept selling iron to the Nazis, and these guys were getting steamed.

Finally, I took him aside. "W.D.P.," I said, "you've got to tamp it down a little bit. These guys are big. They'll kick the shit out of us if you keep insulting their country."

I don't remember his response, but it was something belligerent. Still, he did manage to slow down the barbs, and we kept on playing. It was a cold, rainy, windy day, which made Sir Henry's port especially welcome. So we were at the sixth hole having a few when old W.D.P. said, "I say, they tell me you've played a bit of rounders." His tone implied that he considered the British version of baseball a bit of a sissy game.

"That's right," I told him. "I have."

"You know, I've seen one American game of rounders in my life."

I took a sip of port. "Well, W.D.P., let's hear about it."

"In 1960, we were in Pittsburgh," he began. Immediately, I started looking around, thinking someone had put him up to this, that he was going to talk about the seventh game of the Series that year. But then

I thought, well, his business is steel, so it's logical that he was in Pittsburgh. Someone probably took this visiting foreigner out to Forbes Field to show him what America's pastime was all about.

Ralph and legendary basketball coach Ted Owens at the Field of Dreams fundraising event in Claremore, Oklahoma, 2016."

"We played our eighteen holes in the morning at Oakmont," he continued, "and then U.S. Steel, our host, said we must make haste, because we were going to see one of America's classic sports events, the seventh game of the World Series."

No shit, I thought but I didn't say anything. This was too much to believe. Still, I had to hear it described from this Englishman's point of view.

"Well," he said, "Forbes Field, I believe t'was called. We arrived, and the place was absolutely mobbed. Then, in the final inning, this bloke hit it clean out of the lot, and sheer pandemonium broke loose. We were lucky to escape with our lives." At this point, his eyes got real big.

"You know, W.D.P.," I said, "somebody had to bowl it up there to that bloke."

"Yes. Yes. Of course."

"That was me. I threw the pitch."

He regarded me for a moment. "Oh," he said. "What a coincidence. More port!"

A dozen or so years ago, I was out at the Phoenix Open and met a French pro named Jean van de Velde. In 1999, after going into the finish as the clear tournament leader, he'd lost the British Open Championship at Carnoustie, Scotland—on the final hole. He only needed a double-bogey to win, but he hit a post in the bleachers and the ball kicked into a hazard. If it had gone into the bleachers he would've had a free drop. As it was, it was in the rough, and his club got tangled up in the next shot, which sent his ball into the water. He got it out, took a penalty, triple-bogeyed the hole, and ended up losing to Paul Lawrie in a playoff. If he'd shot a double-bogey or better, he would've been the first Frenchman in 90 years to win the British Open.

It was a spectacular and unfortunate finish for him, but he hung in there and was competing at Phoenix when we met. As a PGA professional,

I had a card that got me into the practice area, and I ran into him there, practicing his putting and chip shots.

I went over to him. "Jean," I said, "do you have a moment?"

"Yes?"

Introducing myself, I told him, "I'm a PGA pro now, but before that I was a baseball player. I played for the New York Yankees, and in 1960 I pitched in the last game of the World Series. I threw a pitch, the guy hit a home run off me, and we lost the World Series. After that, I was America's goat."

Just about everybody in the world has heard of the New York Yankees, of Joe DiMaggio and Yogi Berra and Mickey Mantle, so I was pretty sure he had an idea how important that loss was.

"But," I continued, "a couple of years later, I got into the same situation—the last inning of the seventh game of the World Series. And this time, Lady Luck smiled on me, and I won. Being the goat before just made that victory all the sweeter.

"You just may get another chance to win the British Open, and fortune might smile on *you* then, too. If it does, take it from me: It'll be all the sweeter."

The tears in his eyes told me that he understood. "Thank you for sharing that with me," he said.

I doubt that Jean van de Velde remembers my name. But I hope he'll always remember the day at Phoenix when some old pro walked up to him and offered a little bit of encouragement with a real-life story about second chances.

17

"PLAY HARD, HAVE FUN, AND GET A DREAM."

A lot of times, especially when I'm autographing something for kids, I'll write down a short bit of advice with my signature: *Play hard. Have fun.*

Although I didn't put it into words until much later, I know that those two little sentences have in many ways defined my approach to my careers in professional sports as well as my approach to life itself. It's the way I've gone about my business from the time I was a kid on the Chelsea, Oklahoma, sandlots, and while my sports activity now is mostly limited to golfing with my friends and at charity and celebrity events, it's still the way I do things.

I want to close by telling you about another man with another motto, a former golf pro who managed to triumph over some very adverse circumstances. It will also involve the final story I have about Bill Mazeroski, the Bobby Thomson to my Ralph Branca, the man whose name and mine will be linked as long as people talk about baseball. (I might prefer having Willie McCovey's name come up whenever my World Series performances are mentioned, but that's something out of my control.)

Dennis Walters is this man's name. He was one of the promising young golfers I worked with, but he was more than that. He was like family to me.

One day, when I was out playing at Roxiticus, he showed up at the club, found out where I was, and took a cart out to meet me. But on the way, as he was going down a hill, something happened and his golf cart flipped over on top of him, a piece of the railing on the cart's edge piercing his back and crushing his third vertebrae.

We got him out of there as quickly as we could, and he was soon being operated on, but it was too late. The accident had paralyzed him from the waist down, and there was nothing that could be done to change that. Dennis spent time rehabbing at a clinic in Livingston, New Jersey—the same place Superman actor Christopher Reeve went after the horse-riding accident that crippled *him*—but there wasn't much that could be done for him there, either.

As you might imagine, Dennis fell into a deep depression. He'd had a great future in professional golf ahead of him, and now that dream was shattered. Like his many other friends, I did what I could to pull him out of his funk. He liked baseball, so I got Ralph Branca and Bobby Thomson to sign a ball for him, and then I got Maz to sign one as well. When I put my own signature on that ball, it became a one-of-a-kind item, as I explained to Dennis.

"Maz signed this ball, and then I signed it," I told him. "It's the only time that will ever happen. I will never sign another ball if Bill Mazeroski signed it first; if his name is already on it. If we do a signing together, I'll sign it first and then he'll sign it after me. That's the only way I'll do it from now on. Your collection will have the only one I signed after Maz."

Occasionally, people will come to me with a ball that's already signed by Mazeroski. I'll sign pictures, bats, but I will not sign a ball with his autograph on it. Sometimes people will get a little mad about it, but when I tell them about Dennis and how I told him he would be the only one to have a ball like that, they understand.

Dennis Walters and his dog, Bucky.

Dennis has gone on to put his life back together, and he's done an amazing job of it. He learned how to do trick shots, and he travels with his little trained dog, Bucky. They appear together on the PGA Tour, among other places. In his act, he'll put a tee down, and Bucky will take the ball in his mouth and tee it up for him.

Tiger Woods became a fan of Dennis's back in the early 2000s. Dennis and Bucky were in the practice area at a tournament, and Tiger came down and started petting Bucky.

"Ask him a question, Tiger," Dennis said.

"All right. How many majors have I won?"

Bucky looked up at him and started barking: "Arf. Arf. Arf. Arf. Arf. Arf. Arf."

At that time, Tiger had won seven—so Bucky was right.

Tiger laughed. "All right, then," he said. "How many has Mickelson won?"

Since this was before 2004, the year Phil won his first major, there were none. Bucky communicated that fact by remaining silent and looking up at Tiger, who fell down on the ground laughing.

In addition to his appearances on the golf circuit, Dennis takes his show to lots of other groups and organizations, including schools. He's got a great line of gab and lots of stories, along with a solid message for kids.

"Get a dream," he tells them. "And if that dream doesn't work out, get *another* dream."

That's exactly what he did, and it's worked out very well for him. In addition to all the people he's entertained and inspired over the years, he's been recognized by the PGA of America, which not only presented him with its highest honor, the Distinguished Service Award, but also made him one of only 11 honorary lifetime PGA of America members, whose ranks also include Bob Hope and three former United States presidents.

I'll end this book by combining Dennis's message with mine. Play hard, have fun, and get a dream. I've done all three of those things, and I've been lucky and blessed enough to not only have my first dream of being a big-league pitcher come true, but also to see my second dream, becoming a PGA golfer, come to fruition. Now that I think about it, maybe getting to play another sport at the highest professional level constituted another second chance in my life, just like the 1962 World Series.

From my first major league pitch at Fenway Park to my time on some of the most beautiful golf courses the world has to offer, I've played hard and had fun living my dreams. And no matter who you are, where you are, or even how old you are, my sincere wish for you is that you're busy and happy doing the very same thing.

- o -

Writer and longtime baseball fan John Wooley listens as
Ralph recalls another story from his remarkable career.

THE AUTHORS

RALPH TERRY

The top right-handed pitcher on the fabled New York Yankees teams of the early '60s, Ralph Terry led the America League in wins, games started, and innings pitched in his All-Star season of 1962, collecting a second trophy that year as the World Series MVP. The next year, he again topped all AL pitchers in games started, along with pitching the most complete games. In addition to playing part or all of eight seasons with the Yankees, Ralph's 12-year major league career includes stints with the Kansas City A's, Cleveland Indians, and New York Mets.

After baseball, Ralph turned his attention to professional golf, winning the Midwest PGA Championship in 1980 and competing successfully for years on the PGA Tour and the PGA Senior Tour.

He and his wife, Tanya, reside in Larned, Kansas.

JOHN WOOLEY

Hailing from Ralph's hometown of Chelsea, Oklahoma, John has written, co-written, and/or edited more than 40 novels, graphic novels, and non-fiction works, including the critically acclaimed biography *Wes Craven: A Man and His Nightmares* and the award-winning movie history *Shot in Oklahoma*. His other credits include the made-for-TV movie *Dan Turner, Hollywood Detective* and several feature-length documentaries.

He lives in the Oklahoma countryside outside Chelsea with his wife, Janis.

IMAGE COPYRIGHTS

Every effort has been made to trace the ownership of all the images included in this publication. Any errors that may have occurred are inadvertent and will be corrected in subsequent editions, provided notification is sent to the publisher.

THE NATIONAL BASEBALL HALL OF FAME LIBRARY, COOPERSTOWN, NY
Pages: xii, 26, 46, 67, 84, 95, 98, 101, 123, 125, 131, 139, 142 (*top picture*), 146, 150, 156-157, 158, 160, 166, 176, 177, 235

RALPH TERRY PRIVATE COLLECTION
Pages: 7, 11, 55, 90, 133, 143, 145 (*bottom photo*), 164, 195, 202, 206, 211, 216, 217, 223, 226, 227

JIM RUSSELL PRIVATE COLLECTION
Pages: 6, 165, 236

D. WALTERS PRIVATE COLLECTION
Page: 233

MIAMI TIMES HERALD
Page: 36

INDEX

CPSIA information can be obtained
at www.ICGtesting.com
Printed in the USA
FSOW03n1758161116
27456FS